Date Due

I			the

BRODART, INC.   Cat. No. 23 233   Printed in U.S.A

”

,

Michael Caputo

ISBN: 9781080986927

To the greatest gifts God has given me in Canada: my wife, Leonilda, my children Anthony, Julie and Victor and my grand-children, Ava, Michaela, Daniel and Matthew.

TABLE OF CONTENTS

PREFACE

Every year thousands of individuals and families pour into Western countries from faraway lands and far away cultures. As they are about to step on foreign soil, filled with both hope and anxiety, in all too many cases, their minds are filled with images seen on TV or in movies about rich lands and exciting cities where poverty is nowhere to be found, where abundant wealth is there for the taking.

Unfortunately, those hopeful eyes will soon be confronted with many painful realities. Instead of the large suburban houses, many will end up in crowded apartment buildings filled with criminals, schools packed with young people that will be too self-absorbed to care about them and who all too often see them and treat them as inferiors.

The parents will often go from hopeful to deeply disappointed. The jobs they hoped for will be unavailable to them, and they will have to settle for the scraps that locals do not want and pays that will barely suffice to keep them afloat.

I and my family have been there. We have felt the hope and we have shared in the dreams. I, personally, have felt the abuse – often hate-filled abuse – mentally and physically.

I have seen the hopefulness turn to helplessness in my parents and the temporary discouragement which led to questioning the decision to emigrate and the temptation to go back home where all was so simple, so familiar and so much less challenging.

But I also saw things change. As adaptation took place; as perseverance set in, I saw things improve and I witnessed the benefits multiply – greatly.

As I look back today as an older man from Calabria, in Southern Italy, I remember that all the disappointments, all the challenges, all the anxieties gradually were replaced with surprising adaptation, amazing successes and finally the reaping of wonderful benefits for my parents, who refused to give in, for me who became a successful educator, a psychotherapist and author and for my three children, also successful professionals, who are now part of the fabric of "America," who have at their grasp the many opportunities of this blessed land. All this took place because when things looked bleak and overwhelming their grandparents and father did not give in, and did not give up.

I hope that readers who have recently come to "America" will read and be encouraged not to give in, not to give up, not to allow the feelings of despondency win over their minds, but to go on and continue fighting; for victory and success are ahead, if they only persevere and never allow feelings of hopelessness have their destructive way.

INTRODUCTION

Have you ever heard of Capistrano? No, not the one in California, nor the Capestrano in Central Italy. I am referring to Capistrano in Calabria, a very small town perched on the hills of the southernmost Region of Italy; a small town from where one can behold the adjacent and proud Serre mountains and the stunning Mediterranean right past the green rolling hills which undulate between the town and the blue waters.

Of course you have heard of Montreal and Toronto, in Canada. They are typical North American cities; sprawling, noisy, dynamic and wealthy.

My father decided to transfer from peaceful and idyllic Capistrano – barely two-thousand people – to Montreal, first and then to Toronto, in the late sixties. It sounded like an exciting move we were most willing to undertake, but we had little knowledge of the stresses and strains that such a move would have entailed.

The move was referred to as, "moving to America," totally unaware of the fact that Canada was a country quite distinct from the United States. Since they were both in North America, and the people spoke English, many assumed it was the same location. The fact that a big part of Canada is French speaking was unknown to them and our relatives in Montreal never bothered to inform us that Montreal was a mostly French city in a large French-speaking world.

We had a very idealistic view of "America," in those days. The myth that money grew on trees and the streets were paved with gold was *fairly* present in our minds. After all, when my father and mother were in need, because of an unexpected tragedy, my uncle who lived in Canada sent us money without expectation of return. When my grandmother returned from her stay in Toronto for about nine months, she wore two beautiful, fancy, rich-looking leather boots, more evidence that money abounded in Canada, and my father had a plan to join in to gather some of the bounty.

And there was no doubt in our minds that we would be successful—*fast*. The fields were ready for harvest and my father – who had been quite successful in town – was going to turn our "American" adventure into another success story, with little effort, and within a very short period of time.

This was the hope. This was the dream. But this was a naive dream with weak foundations. Little did we know of the stresses and strains – of the challenges and fears that were awaiting us, that await so many emigrants from all over the world who launch their hopes toward North America and have been doing so for a very long time.

Yes, little did they know that though the North American tree abounds in fruits, it is a very high tree and the fruits are way, way up at the top and the climb is steep and long and sometimes the thorny branches leave cuts and bruises on the skin and that, on occasion, the branches break and the fall can be very painful and for a few just plain fatal.

So welcome to my journey to North America. This time the main protagonist will not be mature adults, though there will be some beside me to accompany me through the, at times, dark valley. The young eyes through which you will see the journey are mine. The images are very much vivid and real, and when they are not I will honestly let you know that details are missing.

I am sharing this journey to once again enlighten my descendents of what it took for them to be in the comfortable situation they are in today, so as to better appreciate what their ancestors who preceded them went through, before they finally reached the top of the tree and started gathering the abundant fruits.

I also intend to enlighten North Americans who were born in this blessed land, so as to help them gain a better understanding of what the awkward foreigners are going through as they get adjusted to a foreign culture, a challenging climate and, at times, not-so-welcoming people who may see them as invaders and robbers of what rightfully belongs to them.

Join me then. See through my eyes, feel through my mind; experience what you may have never imagined before and, thus, grow to appreciate what the "foreigners" go through as they adapt to the land of plenty, before they also start reaping from the tall and challenging fruit tree called by many, "America."

CHAPTER — 1

GOING TO "AMERICA"

My father, Antonio, was born to achieve. He had little education, but he always had big dreams. He was the son of a poor farmer who eked a living from two small plots of land on the side of two adjacent hills. My father's three brothers had little education as well, and one had none. My father was very different. Unlike his brothers who were content with their meager Calabrian life, my father wanted to break free and build and build and build.

And build he did. In just a few years, he built a very successful barber shop, a clothing store and two taxis. He had shown that coming from one of the poorest families in town and having little education did not have to make you a slave to poverty forever. Life had to serve you, not you life. His view was that, if you dream big, work hard and never give in to the challenges of life, you will finally achieve your dreams. But never stop. *Stopping is not allowed.* You keep on climbing and if you have to move to another hill to achieve your dreams you do so and his next hill was going to be either Canada or Australia.

My mother craved to go to Canada. Her three brothers and one younger sister were all located in Montreal and were doing well. My father was willing to also entertain going to Australia, but only if Canada closed its doors to him. But Canada did not close its doors and Australia lost the fight.

The day came when my father had to announce the agonizing news to his mother Grazia, a very old and very loving woman. Upon hearing the news, she fell into the deepest depression. I remember going to visit her more than once, the week preceding our departure and each time she was sitting on a small chair in the middle of her bedroom crying like a fountain. This must have lasted the whole week, as I saw her in the same position doing the same thing, each time I went back.

My mother also announced the news to her mother, but she was a stoic kind of woman who felt pain, no doubt, but quickly accepted the painful reality and repressed her anguish…to cope.

This is what precedes the departure of those strange immigrants that populate our city streets; that are forced to travel on our buses during cold winter days; that crowd the poorer parts of our cities: anguish — profound, heart-wrenching aguish. Anguish that lasts and lasts and mental wounds that rarely fully heal in the minds of the ones who depart and of the ones that are left behind.

THE DAY OF DEPARTURE

One day in June, 1967, as I was playing in the foyer of the Palazzo Brizzi, where the middle school was being hosted, my father suddenly and furtively appeared in the entrance and asked me to follow him.

I was confused; it was about midday, school was not yet over and my father had come to school to take me home. He had never done this before and the whole thing was puzzling. I tried to get an explanation, but he walked hastily in front of me and was very evasive. "Be quiet, and just follow me!" he said firmly.

We walked hastily down the Corso; we crossed the

empty square and within a few minutes we were home. Then the news: the time had come to leave for Canada.

The big cardboard suitcases were ready. My few clothes had been packed. I quickly made sure the ancient coins I had found not long before were safely stowed away, as well as my extensive stamp collection. We would have been driven to the Saint Eufemia train station on a 60's Fiat minivan.

I made sure my treasured coin and stamp collections were well protected as well as well as my paperback Bible my brother-in-law had given to me. Once these treasures were well stowed in a safe location, I was ready for the trip.

The neighbors were informed at the last minute and the news spread like wildfire. Antonio, the barber, Teresa and Michele were leaving for America. A large group of town's people gathered to give their emotional goodbyes. I promised my best friend I would have written; I told the others I would have returned. Then off we went, and on to my newest adventure.

"We crossed the empty square." The piazza, as it looks today.

The emotional goodbyes took place in Four Corners.

THE AMAZING TRIP BEGINS

I looked behind me, as the car was leaving my beloved town. I waved goodbye to my friends, from the back seat of the car. We slowly drove north, leaving behind the centre of town where my house was located. I saw the meandering valley on my left, the Rocca Mountain and the Mediterranean Sea, far away in the distance. We passed Maestro Fera's house, the ever-running Batia Fountain, my Nonna's house and then the last house…

My father had given his emotional farewell to his mother in the morning and dared not stop to see his devastated mother again.

The twisty road took us to Monterosso, the nearby town. We wound our way through the busy streets and, as we were leaving the town, from the back window I saw Brunina, a gracious young lady and school friend from my town, walking down Monterosso's main street with her mother. She was the last friend I saw that day. She did not see me, and I wish she had, as she was a dear childhood friend. I knew it would have been a very long time until I would have seen her again.

We traveled down the valley; passed Monterosso's

cemetery and on toward the Angitola Lake. We rode beside the recently-created, artificial lake and then passed beside the Rocca Angitola Mountain, on our left. I looked up the steep mountain for the last time, and we quickly traveled down to the St. Eufemia Plain, adjacent to the Mediterranean Sea where, within minutes, we reached the area's main train station.

The train trip is a blur. I do not recall how long it took us to get to Naples, or any details surrounding the trip. Most of it must have been a night trip.

My next memories are of the harbor building in the port city of Naples. Its main hall was crowded with old, wooden benches and hundreds of people waiting to board the gigantic ship nearby. Not far from the port, I do remember seeing an impressive castle with very high walls, and the lofty Vesuvius in the distance. Then the unforgettable trip began.

We boarded the Cristoforo Colombo liner, one of the major passenger ships in the Italian fleet. It was huge and swift and it would have taken us to our destination in about nine days. The ship was filled with Italian emigrants and many American and Canadian tourists who were returning home from their trip to "Romantic Italy."

I can never forget the ship's gradual departure; the hand waving from the peer; the picturesque harbor and the majestic Vesuvius; the gradual disappearance of the city of Naples. As Italy was disappearing on the horizon, I must have felt deep sadness mixed with a longing for the promising and exciting unknown in America.

My family was assigned to a round dining table for the whole trip. We shared the table with a lovely Italian-Canadian woman and her two children: a pretty, short-haired girl about my age and her lively younger brother. They had gone to visit family back home, while the dad had stayed back in Canada to work.

The trip was pleasant and exciting, for as long as we were traveling over the placid Mediterranean. The ship was filled with beautiful halls; the lounging areas were spacious and comfortable. Movies in English were being shown in the evening for the English-speaking tourists. I heard the tourists laugh a lot, but I was not interested. Most of my time was spent with the young fellow I ate with, or simply looking at the deep-blue sea stretching out into the endless horizon.

Within two days, the majestic cliffs of Gibraltar appeared on the horizon. I stared at all the visible details of the steep, stony mountain, storing the wonder in my mind to this very day.

About two days after passing by Gibraltar, I was again mesmerized by two Azores islands we passed between. The one on the north side was covered with gloomy clouds and looked rugged, dark and mysterious; the one facing it, on the south side, looked like an enchanted isle from a fable book, with countless terraced gardens climbing up a mountain, spotted by sparkling white houses and churches. Then, more ocean…

After the Azores, the trip felt long and tiring. Ahead were four more days of gray-blue waters and cloudy skies. It was during this phase that nausea set in, and it prevented me from even looking at the water. I was forced to spend my time inside the ship, which I gladly did, so as not to feel nauseous.

I shared the cabin with an older Italian emigrant who was also going to Canada. The man was quiet and strangely aloof. He asked little of me and I reciprocated gladly.

After the four dreary, tiring days…finally land!

Before entering the Halifax Harbor, we passed by many small, rocky islands covered with evergreens. The ship moved slowly, as it approached the harbor. Finally, we reached our longed-for destination.

CHAPTER 2 —

FINALLY ON

CANADIAN SOIL

The harbor looked old and unappealing. The ship finally stopped near the pier. We left the ship, tired and hopeful and finally rested our feet on the land called Canada. The location was the now-famous, "Pier 21." We were then directed to a very large building.

Once inside the building, I saw the Customs' officials on my left, as they were opening the packed, large trunks the immigrants were bringing along. We saw clothes, salamis and plastic jugs of olive oil being taken out. We heard the uniformed officials trying to communicate with the newcomers. There were questions asked and justifications offered, but neither side really understood. Some food may have been kept; most was mercifully allowed to go on. I was a noisy and chaotic sight.

Afterwards, we entered a large hall with a very high ceiling. The floor was lined with wooden benches, as in Naples, but the hall was larger and it allowed more space between them. We sat on the first set of benches, as my father tried to sort out where we would get our luggage.

We had no food and the trip to Montreal would have been long. We went to a small convenience store, beside the huge waiting hall and, at the bottom of a shelf, we found strange-looking bread in plastic bags. It was white, square and it was cut into many slices. By pressing the bag, one could tell that it was also "very" soft. My parents were puzzled by the staple and giggled. I was intrigued. Little did we know how much of that strange–looking bread we would have eaten in the future.

Because there was no other kind of bread, my father bought it anyway. He also bought either sliced meat or cheese and we were ready for the next part of our journey.

While in the hall, something happened that I will never forget. As we were sitting on the benches, a beautiful, tall lady, probably in her forties, dressed in a dark-blue uniform, slowly approached me, took what I vaguely remember to have been a lollypop out of a small basket and gave it to me. Her face exuded warmth and kindness and made me feel very welcome. The lady, in a way, was symbolic of the nation that would have become my adoptive mother – and I felt reassured. Her memory is chiseled in my heart.

The trip on the old and decrepit train was far from comfortable. The night came quickly and so did the cold. It was June and yet the night air was strangely cold like our month of March. Late at night, a uniformed, older man walked by, and my father stopped him and acted as though he was shivering. The man understood, smiled and went to turn on the heating. The rest of the night was comfortable and restful. He was also a kind-looking human being.

We traveled the whole night and part of the next day. The train was slow and stopped many times. The trip must have taken 24 hours, as we reached Montreal late the next day.

Exterior of Pier 21, in Halifax, Nova Scotia. A great many, Canada-bound immigrants landed behind this building. (Photo by, Skeezix1000)

IN THE "BELLE PROVINCE"

Once in the main station in Montreal, we left the train all excited about the nearing reunion with family members I had never met before. Soon I would also see again my beloved aunt Maria, Zio Saro and my dear cousins Rocco, Palma, Mary and Michelina, I had seen depart for Canada years before, and Tony and Alba, born to my aunt while in Canada.

We took the escalator – something I had never seen before and rode on it to the main floor. There we met my uncle Domenic and his wife, Zia Raffaela, an exceptionally warm and loving woman. My uncle Domenic was young, friendly and confident.

We climbed on a very large sixties car and left the train station. We may have gone immediately nearby to my aunt Maria's and uncle Saro's house in one of the older parts of downtown Montreal, named Saint Antoine, near downtown Montreal. We were later met by bubbly Zio Filippo, Zia Lisa and their two children, Mike and Josephine.

We lived there about a month, while my father underwent a barber's test, so as to start working in his profession. I believe he was helped by an Italian man who had a leading position in the Barber's Association. He learned a few basic French and English expressions and then found a benevolent older, English-speaking employer who gave him the opportunity to practice his trade.

While there, I had to get used to a new kind of panorama; not the beautiful green valleys and the mesmerizing Mediterranean – a testimony to God's greatness – but tall and proud skyscrapers, a testimony to human ingenuity and pride.

That summer my cousins and I visited the nearby skyscrapers often. We especially liked visiting them on the weekend, when very few people were around and when we could safely slide down the long armrests of the escalators, without attracting adult attention. We also enjoyed going up and down Place Ville Marie's elevators, but that activity came quickly to a halt when, one day, we were firmly asked by a security guard to leave and not return.

I became very close to my newly-found cousins. They all had very original personalities: Mike (the oldest), uncle Domenic's son, was the leader and we often followed him in getting ourselves into new adventures–and some trouble. Mike (the second oldest) my Uncle Filippo's son, was very bright, and had a way of reinforcing the oldest Mike's adventurous spirit. Little Rocco, the youngest of the group, was bright and vivacious, but was compelled by his age to simply follow along. Josie, my younger, lovable cousin, inspired much teasing. Julia was from youth an unbelievable dynamo. Little Rocky was born, not long after our arrival. He was a gorgeous child, with energy and spunk that stayed with him to this day.

MOVING TO VILLE EMARD

Though we were kindly welcomed by my aunt Maria and her husband uncle Saro, it was understood that we had arrived to Canada to provide for ourselves not to sponge off of relatives, so we soon found a first-floor apartment in Ville Emard, a suburb of Montreal. It was a very small but welcoming apartment situated right across a take-out restaurant with a high pillar holding a big turning bucket. It was named, "Kentucky Fried Chicken."

Many people went there to savor their delicacies, but I do not recall ever going there to buy anything. Why pay when my mother prepared excellent food at home?

Unfortunately, we did not move to the Italian Ghetto in Montreal North, or Saint Leonard. That would have made my first impact with North America a lot less traumatic, as I found out later in Toronto.

The area we moved to was mostly a French-Canadian section of the city with just one Neapolitan family living nearby. They had a robust boy of probably 15-16 who spoke very good French and was limitedly accepted by the area boys. He lived on the fringes of the group and the local gang had no problem being aggressive toward him, as I once witnessed, if they felt the desire to. His name was Fiore.

My mother insisted that I dress well. We had owned a clothing store and some of the best clothes were brought with us to Canada. One such piece was a very attractive vest made of a smooth and rich-looking, velvety brown material. The kids in the area noticed it and assumed we were rich visitors who had come to visit Expo 67 and then return home. Expo 67 was a space-age, international exhibition that celebrated Canada's 100th anniversary, was attracting a great many to the city. That incorrect conclusion had made me taste a level of respect, which I had not tasted before and dared not tell them the truth that we were there to stay.

In time the local kids realized that we had stayed too long and that we were simple immigrants and the change in attitude became palpable, but not in all. I remember a French boy who remained friendly, as well as a pretty young lady who continued liking me as well.

Beside the KFC restaurant, we also were blessed to be beside a very fine park with tall swings and lots of deep sand all around. My cousins and I loved to push the swings as high up as possible and then jump off as the swings before they reached their highest point. The competition revolved around who would jump off and land the farthest. I, somehow, perfected the best technique and became unbeatable without ever breaking a bone. One day an adult saw me fly off the swing and yelled in horror believing that I had accidentally fallen off. The person was reassured when he/she saw from the distance that I was perfectly fine.

South of us one could walk to a major street abounding in stores, supermarkets and banks. They also had a cinema which showed Italian movies about superheroes, but in French. My mother's favorite place was a bakery where they sold packs of expired doughnuts which she would bring home for our consumption. I, unfortunately, ate too many of them, though I did not gain any weight.

Soon the small apartment became a cozy home. My parents bought a very nice-looking black and white TV, which I watched frequently, while indulging in milk, cereal and doughnuts.

The milk was brought to us by a faithful milk man who left the milk bottle in a box in the wall which opened both ways. There he would find the money for his goods, which he would take before leaving the delicious, fresh, white milk.

That was an amazing luxury, but we also had a big fridge – not a puny one which we had back home – and unlike the one back home which had almost nothing in it, the Canadian fridge was full of food my mother bought weekly. Finally we could enjoy an abundance of everything, including different kinds of meats, which had been very scarce back home, because of the exorbitant prices.

Other wonderful benefits were a large sofa which opened into a comfortable bed – my bed – and hot running water for washing dishes and for taking showers, a rarity in our town. We did not have a dish washer, but we must have had an old-style washing machine which, to my knowledge, no one in our town possessed. Best of all, no matter how cold it got outside, the house was always heated, something we have never enjoyed before. The days of freezing-cold winters were over. The time when going to bed in winter felt like one entered a frozen cave had ended and that was a wonderful thing.

Once my father bought his large American car, traveling around in heated comfort made the fierce Canadian winter much more bearable. Thanks to the new car, visiting relatives and friends became much easier, as was shopping in area supermarkets. The only problem that remained was my mother's daily crucible of having to go to work by foot, in hot and cold weather and in the rain.

Weekends were joyful. That was the time when we would visit Aunt Maria's house where the large family seemed to love congregating. I loved my cousins and I loved being with them. I loved Rocco who had been my best friend until he left Italy years before. I loved Palma, Concetta, Michelina, who had been like my little sisters when growing back home and sweet Alba and gentle Tony who were born in Canada.

I also became very attached to Mike, the oldest, son of Zio Domenic, Mike the second oldest, and Zio Filippo's son, joined us to get into mischief quite frequently. I loved teasing Pina and Giulia, also my younger cousins, who had their own very original, lively personalities. And I loved holding little Rocco, Zio Domenic's youngest, who must have been one year old, who by his lively manners promised to grow into a livewire – and he did.

If there was a joyful time, being with my large family certainly provided it. We kidded around. We played the simplest of games around the table and found joy in everything. That was my family – *my blood* – and, thus, they were a part of me and my love for them abounded.

As soon as my parents could do so, they sponsored my sister and her family. The process was fast, and they arrived in Canada within a year. They moved into an apartment about twenty minutes away from us. Finally my nephews Saverio and Tony were with us as well. The joy was complete. Nino and Lucy were yet to be born.

Family is the true safety net for immigrants. Family sticks together. Family members help each other. They help other family members find jobs and are there to offer support, when life gets tough. Yet, some immigrants come here without a family. For them the initial years must be incredibly difficult, but most of them, too, survive.

What also helps a lot are the friends from back home. Within the immigrant communities there are countless sub communities of people who originate in the same towns. They help each other as much as they can, but the family is the sacred pillar that holds you up and the foundation on which you can rest safely and that is one of the great reasons why so many immigrants survive the first years of adaptation and why so many do not return home.

That is why it became mutually beneficial for immigrants to immediately sponsor other family members, to join them and to create another strong nucleus that would make life so much more bearable.

CHAPTER 3—

THEN HATRED AND VIOLENCE

I had been involved in two fist fights back in Capistrano. One with a close friend and I do now know why. We treated his black eye by applying a cold coin and went back to being good friends again.

The other one was more vicious. The boy I fought against was angry and nasty. The poor kid had lost his father in a tragic event and probably carried much anger and mental turmoil in his soul. As I recall, he started the fight, and I quickly won. I remember giving him a bloody nose which only served to enrage him. We were separated by adults, but I doubt we ever made up. His look of fury I never recall being replaced with forgiveness.

By and large, though, the kids of my town were close and fights rarely broke out. We only wanted to play soccer together and have fun, which we did almost daily.

But Montreal was different. We had landed in a sea of French people who had been living together for centuries. There were English areas as well, but they stayed in their own enclaves. The Liberal government had opened the doors to immigration and tens of thousands of Southern Italians poured into the city creating anxiety and resentment in the local French population.

They had lived with the English for centuries and had learned to co-exist, but the Italians were seen as invaders and, thus, they were resented and strongly disliked. The strong resentment in many of the parents was clearly seen in their children. The hatred was also seen in their readiness to start fights with us and the look in their angry eyes, which reminded me of the angry kid back in town who despised every ounce of my being.

For the first time in my life I felt different. I felt hated by all. I felt ostracized and unwanted. I felt what many kids of other colors felt and feel. I tasted racism, and I tasted what it means to be loathed by fellow humans – humans who were of the same color, who spoke a

similar language and who had the same religion. I also felt my whole being fill up with the same quantity of hatred and the same loathing. They wanted me gone and I, unfortunately, wanted them to disappear as well, with just as much vehemence.

NO PEACE ANYWHERE

My introduction to French hatred of Italians took place in a park not far from where my older cousins lived. We had gone there to waste time and just enjoy the swings. Suddenly we were surrounded by an aggressive and large group of local kids. They demanded that Mike, the oldest, participate in a fight against one of their toughest kids. They made a circle and then watched the brutal fist fight evolve. I was kept out of the circle and just sat on the swing overwhelmed by the surreal sight and the brutal loud inciting to violence.

My cousin Mike was a tough, unrelenting fifteen-year-old. He must have put up a vicious fight and must have impressed the demonic crowd. He emerged without a scratch, no bleeding nose and no black eye. The group probably left humiliated by Mike's determination and forcefulness. Mike looked proud and satisfied.

That was the beginning of sorrows—just a taste of things to come.

FIGHTS ALL OVER

Back in my heavenly town, I could go out any time and be met by young friendly faces and much fun. Soon I found that that was not the case in Montreal. Wherever I went, local kids would quickly spot that I was a despised, foreign kid and they would immediately provoke me into a fist fight.

One day I had gone to enjoy the local indoor pool. As I was leaving the pool a boy, a bit taller than I, spotted me and decided to start a fight. To do so, as I was walking, he intentionally put his leg out to make me fall, and I reacted with anger. He instantly invited me to a fist fight in the shower area and the vicious fight began. I was quick at evading his fists and finally hit him in the nose causing profuse bleeding. That, I did not want to see happen, and I stopped. I told him "enough!" but he, instead, took the opportunity to punch me as hard as he could on the side of my face. I still remember the power of his punch and the hatred in the boy's eyes.

He then left and within minutes a swarm of boys appeared ready to exact vengeance for what had happened to their gang member. To leave the swimming pool I turned to a policeman who happened to be nearby who threatened the crowd and somehow, while he was doing so, I was able to escape and run home. While going home, I realized that in the new land, I wasn't just fighting individuals, I was fighting a whole people who hated me and wanted me gone.

I had three more fights. I decided that the best way to prevent the same enraged response was to use a different approach. I was going to quickly grab them by the waist or the legs, I would push them down and then I would hold them down until they would be forced to surrender.

I used this technique successfully when surrounded one day by about 6-7 French boys and was ordered to fight one of them.

I quickly grabbed the boy by the waist and pushed him down. Once he was down, I was determined enough to keep him down. One of his buddies became very angry at his friend's defeat and came at me kicking me in the side. Fortunately he was prevented from continuing by the leader, and I was allowed to go free.

A very similar situation occurred another day, as we were returning from a fishing expedition to the nearby St. Lawrence. That time me, and I do not recall who else, were surrounded by probably 5-6 English-speaking boys who also demanded a fist fight. My technique worked magnificently once again, but there was no rage in those boys. The leader simply admitted that I had won, and he ordered the group to let us go. We left without any further provocation.

That time I felt no hatred, and I saw no rage. I experienced the English fair play and respect for strength for the first time.

Of course the English side saw us as allies in the protection of the English language and were also a minority within the French sea. They did not see us as invaders and, thus, did not have any reason to resent us.

My luck came to an end one day while walking down a major street with my little cousin Rocky. Two much taller boys immediately provoked us and demanded a fist fight. In looking at their size, I should have immediately declined and gone away, but in my pride and self assurance I foolishly decided to accept the demand certain that within seconds I would have knocked him down and would have again pinned him down as I had done with the others.

Unfortunately luck was not on my side that day. I did grab him by the legs and did push him down and my plan almost succeeded, except that while falling his body landed against the outside stairs of the nearby house which led to the second floor and he grabbed to the railings and was able to quickly prevent the fall. He then instantly started pounding me with a volley of well-directed punches to my face and, after having done his sadistic job, he and his buddy jumped on their bikes and ran away.

There was no help to be had from the people who saw the event. I, totally confused and dumbfounded, tried to get someone to call the police but in vain. They probably knew the boys and were not going to betray them. I finally climbed a fence of a nearby park and went to apply cold water on the bruises which seemed to have done the job of preventing any facial inflating, as I do not recall any frantic reaction or severe rebuking from my parents when I went home.

That event was the last fight I was involved in. I do not recall any more provocations, most probably because our stay in Montreal ended soon after.

How many young people who move to other shores have to tackle the same amount of abuse and the same amount of hatred? Some may fight back and become

hardened by the experience. Some, no doubt, who may have a more gentle and sensitive predisposition, may simply withdraw into themselves and suffer in silence. Some may actually stay in their dark hole and never come out. Many join gangs of the same ethnicity where they can find safety and protection.

CHAPTER 4 —

TIME FOR CANADIAN SCHOOLING

September arrived and it was time for school. I had finished grade 8 but not successfully. I did not get to go to summer school because of our June departure. Knowing that we were going to Canada may have led to a slack attitude.

I was sent to Holy Cross intermediate school, a dark-brick, English school. Because they had no English-as-a-second-language classes as they do now, I was put back in grade six to give me time to learn English. Within a few months, someone must have concluded that the decision was a bit drastic and so they put me in a grade seven class instead.

I had a thin, bright and kind black teacher. His last name, "Mr. Liquorish," was not particularly flattering, but his gentle approach was memorable.

The poor man had a fairly large class to worry about and did not know how to help me, so as to prevent boredom from setting in, he asked me to draw Christmas decorations in the library, so as to decorate the cafeteria.

I simply enlarged pictures he probably gave me and turned them into very nice works of art. It was then that the boy from Calabria that he, in fact, could draw impressively well, and that's when I fell in love with art.

I learned very little English that year, except for what I could figure out by listening to my cousins and by watching TV. Fortunately I had studied French in Italian schools, and I could hold my own when going around Montreal.

This was a humiliating and painful time. Being placed in a class of grade 6's at the age of 14 was most degrading. Even being brought up to grade seven within a few months and being only two years behind was hard to take. What helped to hide the painful reality was the fact that I had not developed much yet and was as result fairly short. Nonetheless, I continued being two years behind throughout high school and the embarrassment stayed with me throughout.

Fortunately, today ESL classes abound in many schools and that helps to accelerate English proficiency – but not that much. For the first two or three years many foreign students have difficulty being successful in academic classes and, thus, suffer with the same kind of inferiority complex I tasted for years. Some may become overwhelmed by the experience, lose confidence, quit school early and go and get a factory or menial job when they have the potential to do so much more. I know it happens. I saw that happen to some very bright friends, as I will explain later.

CHAPTER 5 —

MY PARENTS' INITIAL CRUCIBLE

My mother had managed our clothing store quite competently for years. Suddenly she was in another land unable to communicate in either French or English. She was eager to go to work, though, and soon found a job in a toy factory about a twenty-minute walk from home. Her job was to simply wash dolls' faces.

Though the factory was located at a manageable distance, she gladly walked there every day for as long as the weather was acceptable. Once the brutal Quebec winter began, my poor mother was confronted with having to walk the distance in horrific winter storms with no one to drive her to work and no one to pick her up (there was no bus she could take either). Each winter day was a struggle, but she faced them with incredible resilience. The money must have been rewarding enough for her to continue sacrificing to the extent that she did, and sacrificing she definitely did.

Please remember that my mother – like so many other immigrants – came from an area of the world where snow was almost non-existent. In our town one could go around in winter with just a sweater. Below zero centigrade (below 32 Fahrenheit) was unheard of. Blizzards were just plain incomprehensible.

That first winter must have been particularly cold, as the ice buildup on the windows clearly yelled out. Yet, every day, my mother went out and tackled the elements with a resilience that was nothing short of heroic. The weather was brutal, but the joy of being close to her sister Maria, and her brothers, Filippo, Rocco and Domenico and her several nephews and nieces, made all the gruesome sacrifices worth the effort.

Some days as I drive down major Toronto streets in my heated, comfortable car, and I see obvious immigrants waiting at a bus stop in viciously cold weather, I am

brought back to those unforgettable days, and I truly do feel their suffering. But I also know that someday, if they just hang in there, they too will be able to buy a car, so as to escape the torture of waiting for buses that never seem to come, while freezing-cold winds howl around you and raging snow envelopes you, while you desperately try not to freeze to death.

My father, as stated before, owned three businesses and had people working for him. He came to Canada mostly to please my mother. He could have satisfied his desire for more in less cold and challenging Australia, but he could not bear seeing my mother so far away from family, which she loved so much.

From being a businessman and employing others, his first job was washing dishes in Murray's Restaurant in one of the major streets in downtown Montreal. His job was mostly to place the many dishes in a probably moving dish washer and he would then take them out on the other end. His comment was that the dishes were burning hot. He was forced to start with a menial job because, again, he spoke no English or French and no one would have given him a job as a barber, though his barbering skills were unequalled.

It was probably during this time that my father entered

a phase of discouragement and frustration. One day I saw him very angry. He was fed up with all the barriers he was facing and threatened loudly to go back home. The intensity of his emotions was an indication that the clash with another country, another culture, another language were having a very powerful negative impact on his mind.

Many immigrants go through the same phase: the moment when it all seems just plain insurmountable – just plain too much to handle. The dream of fast success suddenly vanishes and the distressing reality that fulfilling the dream will be very hard – or that it may never happen – sets in. The phase is made less intense by family and friends' support, by being successful and accepted on the job and by having supporting fellow workers and managers. If one encounters ridicule and failure on the job, this phase can become extremely hard.

Experts call this phase, "The Crisis Stage." It follows the "Honeymoon Stage." It is the stage when depression sets in, when a longing for "home" multiplies. Some immigrants experience great frustration, especially if their knowledge of the local language is weak, or if improvement in their language skills are limited. This stage can last months or even several years.

How many immigrants just plain give up and quit and go back "home," at this stage? In the 1970's many Italians did return home, after staying only a few years in Canada; but just a few stayed in Italy as job scarcity or the beggarly salaries quickly convinced them that Canada was not that bad after all.

My in-laws went back as well. My father in law, Vittorio, did get a government job soon after his return, but his salary was a fraction of what he was getting in Canada. After about six months, Vittorio and Giulia came back to Canada and regretted their return to Italy ever since. On my part, I am glad they did return, or I would have never met my beautiful wife, Leonilda, and I would have never had the wonderful children and grandchildren we are now blessed with.

But how many do not return back to their country, simply because they cannot take the humiliation of being seen as a failure by their countrymen or families back home? How many accept with resignation that they will have to accept their difficult lot and perhaps fall into deep depression? Hopefully, not one takes the tragic way out and does the unthinkable, but desperation and hopelessness and humiliation are a horrible burden to bear that some may simply not handle it well and might think of ending it all and go into darkness.

My father's angry and demoralized phase fortunately was short lived. He finally calmed down and went back to fighting life and its challenges, as he had always done before.

He, within weeks, left his dish-washing job and was able to finally go back to barbering. An older gentleman, probably of Eastern European descent, was willing to give him a break. He quickly learned a few basic French terms relating to barbering and did the job to the boss's satisfaction.

But he did not work there for very long. The pay was simply not enough to satisfy Antonio and so, within a relatively brief period of time, he went to work at a fancy barbershop in the suburbs. To do so, he bought a big 60's Chevrolet Caprice, a sign to himself and others that he, too, was making progress and that the climbing to the top had begun.

But that was not his greatest dream. He craved to have his own barbershop, but could not get one, because he could not pass the required test in either French or English. That was agonizing for him, but he refused to let go of his dream. When he was informed that nearby Ontario did not have such a requirement, he made the decision to move there and settled in the city of Toronto where my mother had one brother, which to her would have been sufficient to satisfy her longing to be close to family.

CHAPTER 6 —

TIME TO CONTRIBUTE

Soon after our arrival, my father located the family of some distant relatives who had been in Montreal a very long time. The son, also a barber, had set up a very upscale barbershop, which was always packed with clients. The distant relative could not give my father a job, because he had employees that had worked for him for a long time and who had their own faithful clients. One thing he could do, though, was give me a job – a well-paying job – five or six dollars a week for six days' worth of after-school cleaning.

I had worked before in my father's shop back in Italy. I had learned to be very good at shaving people, and I shaved a

WHEN WE CAME TO AMERICA

great many people, especially when my father was away because of his taxi business. Cleaning a barbershop was nothing new to me, so I embarked on the new job with enthusiasm and expertise.

Every time I arrived at the shop, the floor was covered with large quantities of hair. After sweeping the floor, I would carefully spray clean the top of the cabinets and the mirrors. The sinks had to be made to look shining new. I also cleaned the expensive-looking chairs and made sure that when the barbers returned the place was in tip-top shape.

One thing I noticed which was curious was the fact that the cash register was left opened and that some money was left in it. I never dared touch the money nor was I ever tempted to, and I am very glad I was not.

One day the owner of the shop told me that money was being stolen by someone, and they could not figure out who was taking it. The barbers denied having been the thief and someone suggested that the culprit must have been me. To test out the theory, they left counted money in the cash register every night. Needless to say, what they left is what they found and the owner some time later told me what had taken place, and in fact, he was glad that I – his distant relative – was innocent.

Of course, if I had stolen the money, I would have caused a great deal of embarrassment to my parents, not only for stealing, which I was ordered never to do, but also because I would have reciprocated kindness with evil. Though I had stolen as a child, my mother's harsh response had squeezed that proclivity out of me years before, and I am glad her *painful* approach had been successful.

Young immigrants helping families with part-time jobs is a more common reality than we think. While working in the Malton area of Toronto (a mostly East-Indian immigrant community) years ago as a counselor and teacher, I came across some young, high-school students who were helping their families by going to work almost every day soon after school. One worked until late hours and slept little, so as to help the needy family. As a result, such an admirable young person had little energy left for school each day, after having worked until midnight or later.

Of course, young North-Americans also hold part-time jobs, but I suspect that most of them keep the funds they make for clothing, cell phones and other expenses, while immigrant students tend to contribute to the family fund, as I did.

By the way, the few dollars I made were demanded by my mother at the end of each week. I was expected to contribute to family expenses, but I did get a rich allowance of probably fifty cents a week for my efforts, and I don't remember minding that at all.

CHAPTER 7 —

THE WAY TO SUCCESS

HARD WORK – AND FRUGALITY

My parents' philosophy was simple: to be financially successful, hard work is not enough—one must also be frugal. Though my father was a bit of a spender, my mother was *very* frugal, as are most immigrants that I have known. One of the reasons for immigrants' eventual success is, in fact, frugality.

Frugality in my mother was manifested in various ways. First of all, her department store was mostly the Salvation Army store. There she found furniture, various gadgets and clothing. She also visited very inexpensive stores somewhat like the dollar stores or the Wal-Mart's of today, if second-hand stores would not suffice. The one I remember was the 5, 10, 15 Cents stores which carried a plethora of very inexpensive items.

She was also on guard for specials and she did not hesitate to buy dated food. Immigrants know that the difference between fresh food and food which is a few days old is minimal, but the saving is significant.

My mother also refused to buy expensive meats. Hard meat could be made tender by hammering it over and over with the tenderizing hammer. If she could, she would buy in meat in large quantities and would freeze it and then use as necessary.

Restaurant visits were nonexistent (I went to a restaurant for the first time at about 20-21 years of age, and I remember feeling quite awkward during the experience). The idea of paying others large amounts of money for a meal when you can make your own delicious food was seen by my parents as preposterous.

What my mother did was typical of the philosophy used by a multitude of other immigrants of various nationalities. I have a Ukrainian friend who confirmed that his mother was very much like my mother and that

he learned to be frugal from his mother, as I learned it from my mother.

Frugality led to significant savings and to being able to later buy bigger items which were truly necessary. Frugality was one of the reasons for my parents' eventual success and is one of the reasons why many immigrants eventually reach a high financial plateau.

RESOURCEFULNESS AND SACRIFICE

My mother suffered greatly, so to make her contribution to our family success. Her younger sister Maria and her husband Saro did exceptionally well in just a few years as well, because of their flexibility, their resourcefulness and their willingness to sacrifice.

By the time we got to Montreal, my uncle and aunt had six children. Maintaining such a large family required that my aunt also go to work; but how, with so many children to look after? The thought of going on welfare was unthinkable. They had come to Canada to be a success story not to simply scrape through while depending on government handouts.

Zio Saro had a day job in a factory where my uncle Filippo had worked for a long time. For my aunt to contribute she had to get a night job. Every afternoon, she would wait until her oldest, Rocky, was home from school and then she would leave the family and go clean buildings in downtown Montreal. All the food was ready and my uncle only had to take over the family supervision when he got home.

This they did for years – *gladly*. They were sacrificing for their many children and, therefore, it was all worth it.

Amazingly, my aunt Maria had extended family over almost every weekend and always welcomed us with a glowing smile. She was strong and overflowed with love. She was and still is, *amazing*.

The resourcefulness and spirit of sacrifice paid off. Within a few years they had enough for a down payment and bought a nice house. My uncle Saro decided that he could make much more money by buying houses, fixing them up and then reselling them. This was his weekend job. This approach filled the family coffers and provided abundantly for his large family.

They knew, all along, that just holding a simple job would not have taken them far. They had to go the extra mile – and they did, and the results were impressive.

Thus, by being resourceful and by sacrificing, the

young couple that was barely surviving back home, that lived in a tiny, two-very-small-rooms apartment, that barely scraped through and could very easily have been labeled as being poor, ended up living in a large house, in a prosperous suburb of a large North American city, with plenty of money to spend, able to help their children as they moved along into adulthood, proud of their accomplishments.

I do not know all the sacrifices made by my uncle Domenic, my mother's youngest brother, but I do know that he came to North America in the fifties and that his first job was laying train tracks in Labrador, a very inhospitable part of Canada, heavily populated with bears. At night they slept in the safety of railroad cars. Later on he worked in a lamps factory and gradually worked his way to being a well-regarded manager.

I believe his wife, Zia Raffaela, another very special and hard-working lady, worked in factories as well and eventually accompanied Zia Maria to her night job. They now own a beautiful house, three apartments and land in the country with a small cottage they love to spend much time in.

I do not know much about Zio Filippo's story (my mother's oldest brother), but he and his wife, Zia Lisa, must have worked very hard as well, since by the time we arrived they, too, owned their lovely home and three apartments. Another success story.

My in-laws came from a typical Italian village located on the mountains of Abbruzzi, in Central Italy. Vittorio fell in love with Julia, a very refined local young lady.

Vittorio knew that staying in town would not have provided sufficiently for the family he wanted to form with Julia, so he decided to try Canada.

In 1954 he came to Canada, soon after marrying Julia. Julia followed him nine months later. Vittorio did factory work and, finally, ended up working in a Carrier air conditioning factory where he became an excellent sheet metal worker. He worked in that field until retirement.

Julia had no training of any kind. She started working in factories. Julia had a terrible time adapting to Canada and cried for three months, unable to adapt to the loneliness and the new culture and language.

After working in clothing factories for a few years, she decided to go to hair styling school and became a much-appreciated hair stylist. In time she bought her own shop and did very well servicing a clientele that loved her work.

Hard work, frugality and resourcefulness finally brought them to buying a house in costly Woodbridge, which is where they lived when I met them and their gorgeous daughter, Leonilda, who has been my wife for decades.

The Checcas have also been a success story, like many others who came to Canada with almost nothing but dreams and a desire to do well.

Many immigrants, in the city where I live, are now quite successful. Some people insinuate – especially in regards to Italians – that their success was based on being a part of the Mafia, but in the vast majority of cases it was based on very hard work, much sacrifice and abundant frugality.

In an Internet article on the ten richest families in Canada, two are families of Italian immigrants that came to Canada I believe in the fifties. Hard work paid highly in their case and in many other cases. They are the ones that reached the very top of the North American tree and are eating *abundantly* of its fruits.

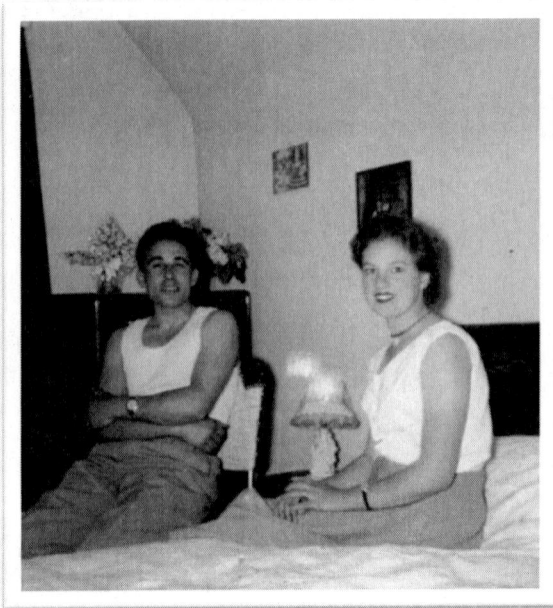

*Vittorio and Julia in their small Toronto
flat, in eager to pursue their Canadian dreams.*

*Zio Domenic and
Zia Raffaela (top
right), who sponsored
my family to come to
Canada. Zia Lisa
(bottom right), and
my parents (top
left).Zia Raffaela's
dad (centre) was
visiting from Italy.*

Zia Maria, Palma, her daughter, my sister, Maria and Teresa, my mother. Zia Maria lives in Montreal but the two sisters did their best to meet as often as they could.

CHAPTER 8 —

ITALY IN CANADA

THE GARDEN OF EDEN—IN THE BACKYARD!

One of the most welcome discoveries once in Canada was the backyard. Of course most Canadians used their backyard to picnic in summer and to plant beautiful plants and flowers. Planting plants and flowers was not an Italian interest, they, instead, quickly saw other agricultural potential.

Most Italians, let us not forget, came from rural areas and were well-versed in growing fruits and vegetables. Once they realized that the Canadian land was quite productive, they got to work to get rid of much grass and plants so as to plant tomato plants and bean stalks. They also planted various vegetables and herbs.

In time they realized that much of their production could be stored in freezers to be consumed in winter, which is what my mother did in large quantities. In fact all winter long I ate her summer bounty: green beans, frozen tomatoes turned into sauce and other goodies that were truly organic and delicious.

I am not a gardener but my wife is. She, like her parents, plants tomato plants, bean stalks, lettuce and other vegetables. The quantity though, is not sufficient to stalk up for winter; nonetheless we do enjoy wonderful organic vegetable during the summer months.

Some went a step ahead and actually planted several fruit trees as well. In my father's backyard there were some fruit trees that produced large quantities of fruits, which they shared with relatives and neighbors.

We, too, had three fruit trees which gave us delicious organic fruits for years. In time our pear tree produced so many pears that it became a challenge to find takers, given the fact that my family could simply not consume all of them.

Some pear trees in our part of the country produce so much that much of the production rots on the ground for lack of takers.

Some Italians went further and bought farms where they could put their agricultural skills to work. Some such Italians ended up building small summer markets on the side of roads, so as to sell their production.

Some went further still. Having found out that the land near Windsor, Ontario, was ideal for growing tomatoes, they moved there and grew tomatoes in great quantities much of which finds its way into cans which are then sold for tomato sauce.

Others moved to the Niagara Peninsula and bought land which they turned into fruit orchards and vineyards. Some of the Niagara wine is produced by the descendents of those entrepreneurial Italian immigrants who loved to stay close to the land instead of working in construction.

My father-in law, Vittorio, lovingly looking after his tomato plants.

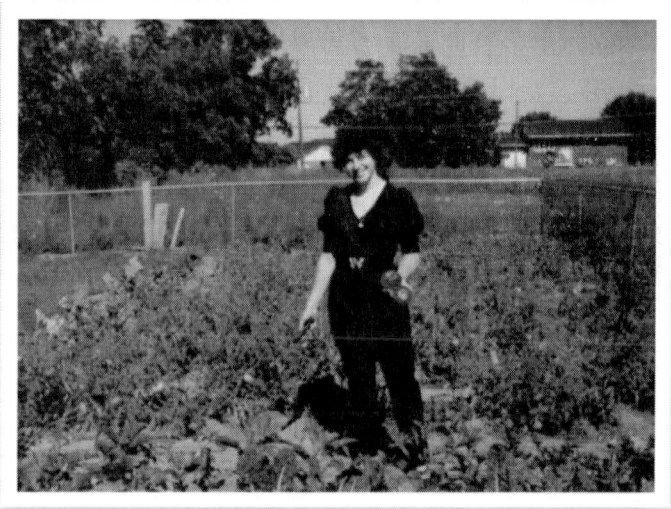

Leonilda, Vittorio's daughter and my wife, follows her dad's example, reaping the bountiful benefits of gardening.

HOME-MADE VINO

Back in Italy, many Italians in agricultural areas made sure they had a small vineyard on their land which they could use to produce self-made wine for the winter months. Some simply bought cases full of grapes and used it to make wine of various qualities.

Here in Canada, some entrepreneurs found that they could exploit Italians' craving for home-made wine and therefore they would import huge quantities of grapes from California, which they would then sell to grateful immigrants.

They also sold all the equipment necessary to make and store the grape juice which, in time, would turn into wine.

Some, like my uncle Rocco, became true, expert wine makers. His ability to make different kinds of wines was nothing short of admirable.

He and a great many other Italian men longed for the arrival of the luscious grapes which they would expertly and lovingly turn into delicious nectar.

Because that generation is almost gone, the mountains of grapes are no longer present, but there are Italian wine stores that still provide all that is necessary for the cultural habit to continue thanks to the children of immigrants that continue following their parents' example.

My father was not a wine drinker, so I did not have any example to follow, except my uncle's. I did attempt to make some wine one year. The results were mediocre. The wine was good for cooking but not for drinking and my somewhat failed attempt did not repeat ever again.

THE YEARLY, SAUCE-MAKING FESTIVAL

What was a longing for Italian men was equaled by a special longing of Italian women: making tomato sauce.

Around the same time when the grapes for wine arrived, mountains of wooden cases filled with tomatoes appeared beside them. They were imported for the hundreds of thousands of Italians that preferred to make their own Italian sauces instead of buying the acidy sauces one finds in stores.

Once bought, they were brought to the garage where they were allowed to ripen while spread out on plastic sheets. The ripened tomatoes were then washed thoroughly and, once they were cut into sections, they were fed into a squashing machine that would turn the tomato into sauce. The sauce would land inside glass jars and, after some basil was added, it was tightly closed and placed in very large pots.

The jars would stay in boiling water for several hours, and when expert eyes concluded that they were ready the boiling would stop and the water was allowed to cool down. Once cool, the jars were stored away in the "cantina," a cool cellar where they were stored for winter consumption.

THE "CANTINA"

You were not a true Italian, unless you had a cantina in your cellar. This was the place where Italians stored various kinds of foods and wine. Home-made salami would be made and then would be hang from the ceiling. Demijohns of home-made wine rested on the floor. The shelves were packed with jars filled with tomato sauce and other preserves.

Canned foods and various kinds of pastas were also bought in large quantities when found on special. The freezers were filled with frozen vegetables and frozen tomatoes from the garden and frozen meats often from the half of an animal they had bought at a discount in an Italian butcher shop or a farmer.

No Italian was afraid of ever running out of food and the sight of an Italian "cantina" left many non-Italians speechless and amazed.

Many from the second and third generation will not buy a house unless there is a "cantina" in it and some who buy a house without one make sure that one is built.

The quantity of food in cantinas has decreased somewhat, but the quantity of food stored in Italian-Canadian cantinas is still impressive. Come and see my cantina and you'll see what I mean…

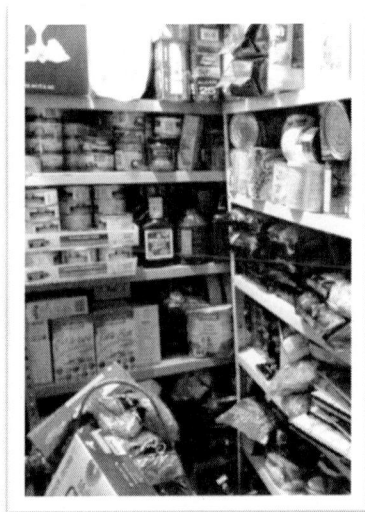

A fraction of a second-generation, Italian-Canadian "cantina."

CHAPTER 9 —

WHEN THE YOUNG BECAME ADULTS

Learning a language after the teen years is known to be a slow and difficult challenge – not so for young people. My young cousin Rocco, who was about ten years of age, was very talented in this area and became proficient in English and French quite quickly. This became a blessing for his family, as they were always in need of a translator, be it in stores, doctors' offices or hospitals. I am sure that he became very beneficial to us as well.

Rocco gained high status in the family, because of his

continual contributions. For years he was, in fact, *essential*. Everywhere he went to translate he received much adulation from the staff for being proficient in both English and French and for his bright and quick mind. In fact in the hospital where he translated for family and friends quite a few times, he was so well known and admired that the staff made sure that a gift was ready for him at Christmas time. There, under the Christmas tree, was for years a special gift for little, but amazing, Rocky.

Young people lose their young status quickly among certain immigrant communities, because of this reality. They are treated as little adults, and they gain a lot of self-esteem, because of the praises and gratitude they earn from the adults that use their services.

It took me a few years to become my family's translator in Toronto. I too became important but was not always grateful for having to regularly make phone calls to various offices or to accompany my parents to various locations to be their translator, as Rocky had done.

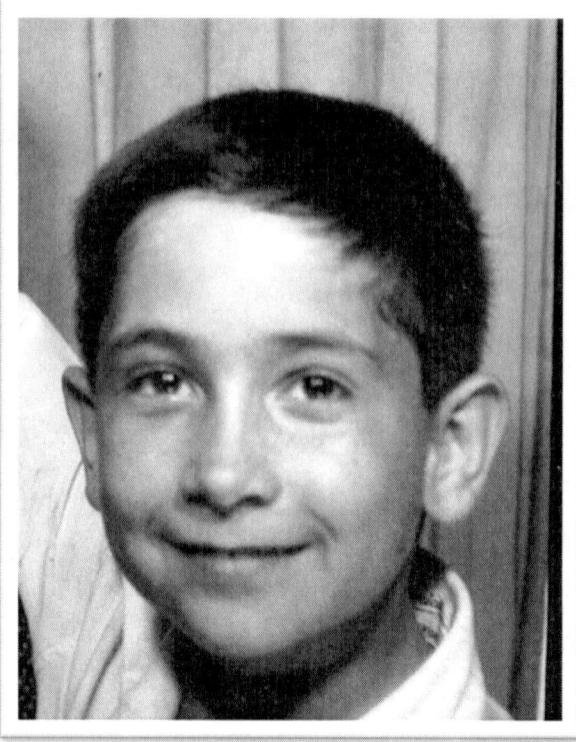

Rocky: Adorable and indispensable for family and friends. Children like Rocky became essential in dealing with Canadian offices and hospitals.

CHAPTER 10 —

ADAPTING TO CANADIAN SCHOOLS

IN HIGH SCHOOL...BUT NOT FOR LONG

As my parents were undergoing their crucible, I was enduring Holy Cross elementary. Afterwards I tackled another challenging summer and then embarked on High School. By then, I had learned some English–but not much.

I went to James Lyng High School, on the edge of Ville Emard, an anxiety-filled day, with my older cousins. We entered a big, crowded hall together, but they soon found which classes they had to go to and disappeared. I was left alone, not knowing where to go. I felt lost and panicky. Someone must have finally led me to the office and somehow I was able to explain my predicament or maybe an Italian-speaking secretary helped me to find my way to Ms. Sweck's class where I was welcomed for the next few months.

Miss Sweck was young, tall, robust and dynamic. She exuded energy, warmth and caring. She, like Mr. Liquorish, wanted to help me learn English, but unlike Mr. Liquorish, she had a few resources: a collection of small books about English grammar which I did my best to read, while Miss Sweck taught her classes, so as not to get very bored.

Amazingly, I impressed the class with my spelling ability, during class spelling competitions. I invariably was one of the most successful spellers. How? You might ask. Because the challenging words being used were words which had a Latin roots and, thus, they were quite easy for me to spell. The moment the teacher used other challenging words which did not have a Latin root, my spelling expertise would come to a grinding halt.

Though the reasons for my spelling success was my familiarity with Latin-based words, I gladly accepted the praise and acclamation from the teacher and the puzzled fellow students. Anything that would feed my shrinking ego was most welcome.

In that school, I never got provoked into a fight. I do remember being taunted once by an English-Canadian boy outside the school, but I stood my ground. The boy laughed at my funny accent and then let me be.

CHAPTER 11 —

ON TO TORONTO...

Like déjà vu, one late fall day, about one year and one half after our arrival, my father showed up at my school, and I was called down to the office. My father had already told the secretary that we were moving to Toronto.

We left French Canada behind and left most of our family behind. I was going to miss the host of cousins I had in Montreal. I had grown to love them all and thoroughly enjoyed our time together. But my Quebec family culture was not one of encouraging university education. If one got a job and worked hard that was enough. My cousins were bright, but they were not particularly enamored with school, except for Mike number two who seemed to be quite promising. Unfortunately, leukemia stole his young life away about one year later. In Montreal I would have probably followed the easy life that my cousins favored and would have not achieved anything in the way of higher education. In that sense, moving to Toronto was a great blessing.

In Toronto I only had one uncle and a few cousins I didn't know.

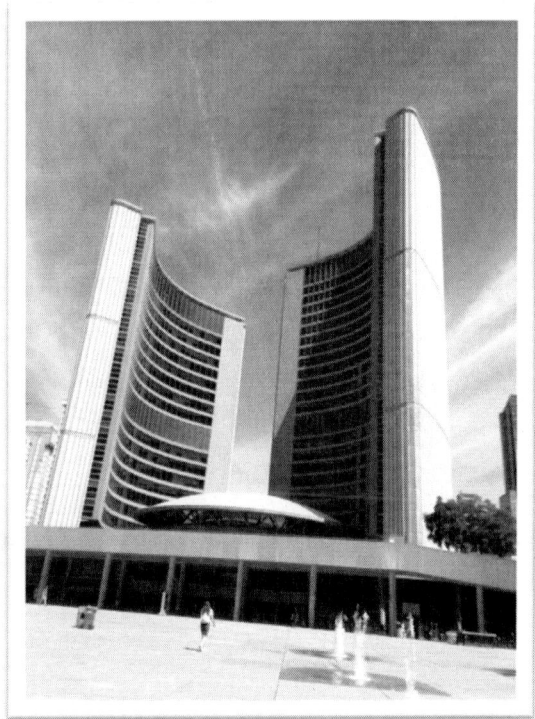

Toronto City Hall: Our adaptation also entailed adjusting to space-age buildings and skyscrapers.

WHEN WE CAME TO AMERICA

AN ALMOST NIGHTMARE

We arrived in Toronto and found that while we had left much snow behind, the weather in Toronto was significantly milder. We settled into our new second-floor apartment and, within days, I was told that an important document was missing. I had to go back to Montreal, go to a specific office and fetch that critical document.

I went back to Montreal by train. I then took a bus and went to the office in downtown Montreal. While on the bus, I experienced my last French-Canadian provocation: a man who laughed at me for being dressed the way I was. I went to the office, got the document and went back to the train station only to find out that the train was going to leave very late, probably because of inclement weather.

The hours passed by, as I sat on a bench waiting for the positive announcement. While waiting, I sat beside a man who seemed to be a decent man. He was staying in the hotel above and was simply wasting time in the station...or was he?

He heard my predicament and offered his couch in his room. I thanked him and declined. Maybe the man was as kind as he looked—maybe not. Psychopaths are

charming and exude trust. He may have been a psychopath looking for a naïve boy he could use for his perverted cravings. I am glad I was smart enough not to fall for the appearance or that may have been a horrendous introduction to another of life's curses: pedophilia.

The train finally left. I arrived at the Toronto station early in the morning, took a cab, and went back to the safety of my new apartment. Another immigrant boy, years later did not have the same luck and paid with his life after undergoing the most horrific treatment on the part of 2-3 psychopaths.

HATED BY MY OWN

Of course, we moved close to my uncle Rocco. There I became close to my other cousins: Mike, Angela, and Palma. Ossington Avenue was on the edge of Little Italy. We lived in the upstairs flat of a house owned by a young family who had emigrated from a town next to ours. The kids were noisy – and *nosy*. Within months my father found another flat just north, on the same street, in an older Sicilian couple's house. From there I daily went to another Catholic middle school. I lived in an Italian area and, therefore, went to a predominantly Italian school. I finally felt safe. Unfortunately, those treasured feelings were shot-lived.

The minority in that school were Portuguese kids. The troublemakers were a small gang of Italian boys led by a depressed and angry young man named Joe, whose parents had died and who lived with his married sister. Joe was tall and strong and was adored by some of the toughest boys in the school, some of which were taking karate lessons.

The most hated boy in the school was a very tall and, based on the salivating Italian girls in the school, a very handsome young man. His misfortune was that he was Portuguese. My misfortune was that I and another boy who happened to live in the same area would walk to school with him every day and back again. The gang assumed that I, too, was Portuguese. Unlike my tall friend, I was short and thin looking, so they decided to vent their frustrations at me.

One day, a vicious young Italian fellow, who happened to have been one of the school's karate experts, decided to practice his flying kicks on me. I was walking alone on the sidewalk in front of the school when, suddenly, I felt a powerful force push at me from behind, and I immediately saw myself flying forward and landing on my arms and face. The force behind the sudden and painful experience had been the feet of the karate expert.

I got up shaken and angry, but he had run away. I do

not recall any gathering of kids. At least in Montreal the fights were face to face. There, *among my own*, I would be attacked from behind. That day I concluded that I would no longer be safe *anywhere*.

The traitor tried to provoke me again another day in front of a group of girls who were in my class, but they came to my rescue and the fight quickly ended. I left humiliated, but leaving was a good idea. His advanced karate skills would have made him very hard to even approach.

That incident, though, was the turning point. The girls informed the boy and his cronies that I was not Portuguese but Italian like them, and from that day forward I was left alone. Amazingly, soon after, the gang opened its arms to me and I became a pal. I was the same person, but my identity had been changed by a new ethnic label and, thus, within moments I had become acceptable. As if by miracle, I went from hated to being loved. My relationship with the karate traitor never healed.

The fact that I later became one of the school's track stars, having won the one-hundred-yard race at the West Toronto track and field championships, made me more than acceptable still. I became a hero – *their* "Italian" hero.

It was this event that made it plain to me that human nature everywhere can be mean and irrational from the younger years. I concluded then that in general humans love to see themselves and their own kind as being superior and that many love to persecute or ostracize others who are not part of their group. The fundamental problem, therefore, was not a French, English or an Italian problem—*it was a human problem*.

While all this was happening, I kept in touch with some friends back home. I missed my friends. I missed the peace and safety of my town. I even missed the boredom in my town, but I especially missed the adventures my friends and I would regularly create together so as to escape the boredom.

Our first Toronto home. We lived on the second floor in a fairly spacious flat. This picture is quite recent. Little has changed, except for the second-floor antenna.

LIFE IN THE ITALIAN GHETTO

Moving to little Italy was a great idea. We felt as though we were living in an Italian island, with Italian neighbors, Italian stores and even three Italian cinemas. In summer, local parks were filled with Italians, and, occasionally, with Italian entertainers who were filling the air with melodious Italian songs. There was even an occasional movie out in the open in the Saint Clair Avenue area.

By the early seventies, the Italian community had reached about three-hundred-and-fifty-thousands and, thus, we had become a force to be contended with. Toronto's Little Italy had become, in reality, one of the biggest Italian cities in the world.

In response to our "invasion," the English-speaking community had mixed feelings. We had been enemies during the Second World War and some still retained the resentment, but as they got to know Italians, and saw their hospitable and warm ways and as they saw how hard they worked and how successful they were, they became less resentful and more respectful.

Unfortunately a few retained their anger and prejudice. The stereotype that Italians are Mafiosi is still lingering on.

The view that Italians become successful because of their criminal associations continues. Some, unfortunately, became envious of our success but that, again, is human nature.

Unfortunately, if you are a Calabrian, now more than ever you are viewed with suspicion, because of the stories people hear about the vicious Calabrian Mafia, and, of course, for some all Calabrians are now Mafiosi, as once were the Sicilians. (For the record, the vast majority of Calabrians are decent human beings that work very hard, raise decent families and are very respectful of others). The few who have chosen organized crime are a curse on fellow Calabrians, as well as others they come in contact with.

PREJUDICE CREEPS IN

In time, the human tendency toward prejudice became an unfortunate reality even among the Italian community. Since they lived in the centre of town, they came in contact with the poorer English-Canadians who would often be on welfare. This led them to conclude that they were lazy and didn't like to work. This, of course, was an unfounded generalization which, gradually, waned as more and more hard-working English-Canadians were met and some intermarrying started taking place.

English-speaking teachers in various schools could see that Italian young people were generally well mannered and respectful. They quickly learned that Italian students feared their fathers and that a call home would have molded the few troublemakers into shape.

In the Italian community, there were no gangs; there were no drugs; there were no secret drinking of alcohol (alcohol was available to Italian kids since childhood and it was not in any way a way to show rebellion).

Slowly suspicion toward people of color entered in, when large numbers of Indians and Pakistanis started moving into Toronto during the seventies. It, though, was based on simple ignorance of the people and their culture and nothing else. When a large number of single, Jamaican mothers and their children moved to Toronto and the news started reporting that some of their teen kids were getting into trouble with the law, some racism started creeping in. Ironically, a number of Italians started reacting toward others as others had reacted toward them.

CHAPTER 12 —

IMMIGRANT LIFE IN TORONTO

I was happy in Toronto. Little Italy became my haven, and I loved to walk down to bustling College Street and savor a totally Italian atmosphere. Italian bars offered the typical Italian drinks, coffees, gelatos and pastries one could find in any part of Italy. Italian music could be heard in the background, as people sipped their espressos or cappuccinos outside the bars protected from the sun by colorful Italian umbrellas.

Fruit stores abounded, as well as "macellerias" (butcher shops). One could find pretty much anything Italian and that felt very heart-warming and reassuring.

Right in the middle of Little Italy was CHIN radio founded by the son of an Italian who had arrived with the first wave of immigrants at the turn of the last century. He spoke Italian with some effort and with a thick accent. But he had hired announcers directly from Italy and they provided all-day Italian programming from a small second-floor apartment where a few studios where crammed together. I saw the location, when one night I worked there as a young security guard.

Neighbors generally got along and helped each other. Visits involved visiting not just family members but also other townspeople who had moved to Toronto. In summer I would faithfully visit a wonderful couple and their children not very far from us, and I was always welcomed as a child. My deep respect for Rita is still intact, and I still call her to wish her a happy Mother's Day faithfully each year. She is still the wonderful lady I knew as a teenager.

Picnics in parks adjacent to Toronto were faithfully visited by swarms of Italians who got together with friends and relatives to enjoy a full day in the country.

Our favorite park became Albion Hills Conservation Area, just north of the upper limits of West Toronto. The hills, the beautiful trees, the stream that cut across and the small pond reminded us of our land and we savored every minute.

Other sought after locations where the beaches of nearby lakes. Some endured the busy Lake Ontario beaches in Toronto. Many sought and found smaller but cleaner beaches just north of the city. The most amazing beach was Wasaga Beach, just about one hour north of Toronto.

The beaches are very large, the sand is fine, the water is clean and one must walk a long way to get to high water. The location was and remains the closest thing to Mediterranean beaches and a great many visit the location daily, during the summer months.

Many happy hours were spent, talking, eating and drinking with relatives and friends, in parks in or near Toronto.

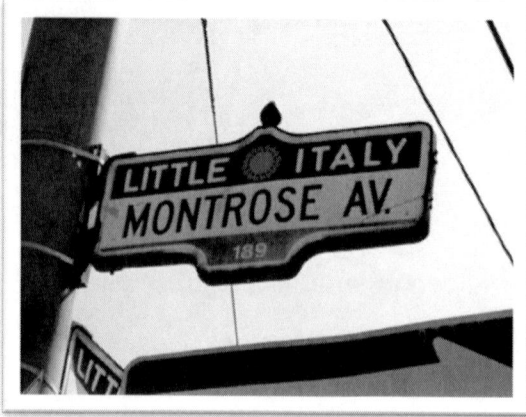

"Little Italy." Most Italians who came to Toronto settled in this general area, or north of it.

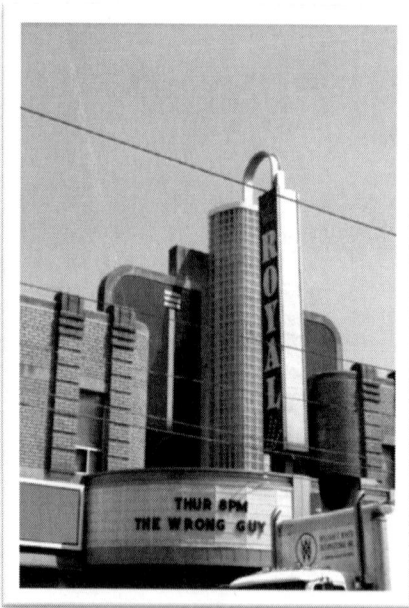

One of four Toronto cinemas where Italian movies were regularly shown.

THEN CAME THE PORTUGUESE...

Not long after Italians invaded Toronto, the government allowed a large wave of Portuguese to settle in Toronto. They were not as many as we were, and they happened to settle right next to us or among us in the downtown area. The Portuguese people speak a Latin language and they are fanatically Catholics, like Italians are. They love their large families and they are very hard-working people. Many ended up in construction, like Italians.

We were very similar, but when the World Cup in soccer took place and the Brazilians defeated Italy in a humiliating final (led by unbeatable Pele'), they were fully supported by the Portuguese who spoke the same language as the Brazilians, then they immediately became adversaries.

The fact that they dared to parade their cars and the Brazilian flags right down College Street was simply too much to bear, and a great many tomatoes and other sundry items flew in their way including an ice cream, which I had bought and which I stupidly threw at one of their cars instead of enjoying it.

It was then that the Italians and Portuguese became opponents and that almost-comical animosity comes to the fore each time the world cup returns and Italy faces off Portugal or Brazil.

By the way, we keep on patiently explaining to our Portuguese neighbors that Brazil is populated by a great many non-Portuguese and that many of Brazil's players are glaringly black and that some players are, in fact, of Italian descent and that the language is the only major thing they have in common. In spite of all this, they stubbornly refuse to accept reality and continue seeing Brazil as an extension of Portugal and no one can change their minds. This of course continues fueling the rivalry between our two communities and a few tomatoes may still fly, occasionally.

CHAPTER 13 —

FACING CANADIAN REALITIES

Just as Canadians were perplexed by our less-than-polite manners (by rigid British standards, that is), our loudness and our willingness to pack more than one family into one small house, we were also perplexed by many Canadian realities we were witnessing all around.

Their intense love for pets and Canadians' willingness to allow pets in the house was hard to comprehend. Their tendency to encourage their children to leave home by 16, or soon after, was to us a sign of callousness and just plain cruelty (Where was the parental love?). Canadians love for sweets instead of fruits was baffling and their lack of familiarity with delicious Italian recipes was inexplicable.

Furthermore, their lack of emotional expression at funerals was most perplexing (Why were they celebrating instead of mourning?). But the thing that was totally impossible to comprehend was Canadians' "rudeness" in funeral homes where they would talk loudly and even laugh while a person lay dead and the family members were in mourning.

All of the above led us to feel quite advanced and our ways quite superior to their ways. We had a heart. We put people first, not animals. We mourned for the dead; *we did not celebrate*. We ate great food, not just meat, potatoes and vegetables. And we definitely did not do the ultimate absurdity: eat *raw* vegetables!

Of course significant changes have taken place over the decades and many of the above traits are now the traits of Canadian-Italians. Our children also love pets – ***and keep them in the house.*** **Some of us tend to nudge our kids to get going – but not too fast – maybe when they hit thirty and they are still unmarried. Fewer emotions are shown at funerals and a few funerals look peculiarly Canadian with people standing, talking and even,**

occasionally, laughing. Many of us eat less Italian food and more meat, vegetables and potatoes and, scandal-of-all-scandals, we have learned to *endure* raw vegetables.

OUR FIRST ENCOUNTER WITH SALESMEN

Not long after our arrival in Toronto, as I was reading a well-known magazine, I came across an invitation to copy the picture of a simple drawing to test my art abilities. I copied the drawing with limited effort and made it quite similar to the original. Excited, I sent it in for an evaluation.

The evaluation came back soon after and it confirmed my artistic talents, which they would have gladly developed through their art course by correspondence. They also added samples of their lessons and the names of successful artists that had been trained by them, including Charles Schultz, the famous cartoonist.

If I was interested, a representative would have come to visit me and explain the missing details. My parents became excited at the fact that I had artistic abilities. They quickly agreed to have a representative visit us and, within a shot while, he was sitting with us singing the praises of the course.

As we understood, it would have been a year-long course, which would have been paid monthly. The amount was not that high. Unfortunately, whether we did not understand or the salesman withheld all the information, the course would have taken at least a year beyond what we had believed and so would have the payments. This fact became clear as the end of the first year came to an end and the course was far from complete.

The venture proved to be costly and taught us a very good lesson. We learned to beware of signing on the dotted line. We also learned to beware of charming salesmen who come to you not always eager to share all the relevant details.

Fortunately the course ended up being quite good, and I did learn some very fine artistic skills that are still with me to this day, yet my growing in art skills put my parents through financial stresses which were not necessary.

Newcomers to North America are choice subjects for scammers and not-so-ethical salesmen. Some or many fall prey to their deceits and end up being scammed of much money yearly, simply because they have not yet learned that North America can abound in fraudulent types just as much as any other place around the world.

CHAPTER 14 —

MOVING AGAIN AND AGAIN...

When we arrived in Toronto in late 1969, we moved into the second-floor flat of a Calabrian family composed of a couple and several children ranging from probably 7-8 to about 14 years of age. The house was right next to College Street, the heart of Little Italy. The flat was spacious but the amount paid was simply too much for my father to accept. We were there a few months and soon moved a few blocks east to Crawford Street into another flat owned by other Calabrians. We again stayed there a few months and again moved back to Ossington, but a few blocks north of the first house we had lived in.

My father, having the heart of a businessman, did not mind moving, as long as it meant paying less money. We moved to a flat of a house owned by a Sicilian elderly couple who were not always very easy to get along. Oh, how the old man loved to brag about having Mafia connections. I remember his sharing with us the story of his initiation into the criminal organization, but I doubt there was one once of truth into his story.

THE GOVERNMENT HOUSING NIGHTMARE

It was somewhere along our travel from house to house that my father became aware of government housing. He applied and somehow was able to get accepted. The maneuver was meant to lead to sufficient saving, so as to have a down payment on a house.

We were assigned an apartment in the toughest government complex in Toronto. Up to that point we had finally experienced the peace of living in our Italian community; then, suddenly, we found ourselves in a rough and scary housing development which comprised 2-3 probably 14-storey buildings surrounded by a very large number of government houses. Though most of the people who lived there were decent human beings who could not afford much, some of the tenants were alcoholics and drug users who caused the local police station a lot of grief. We happened to end up right across an aggressive alcoholic and his family.

For some strange reason, the small balcony was shared with the people who lived next door. We shared it with a decent couple while the alcoholic neighbor shared with probably another alcoholic. I remember the constant fights between the man and the woman next door and the yelling which seemed to never end. I also remember the very loud fire alarms which kids or drank adults loved to turn on to the agony of us sane tenants.

One day I heard loud yelling in the hallway. I foolishly opened the door to see what was going on. One of the participants was the alcoholic who lived right across from us. He immediately turned my way and focused his fury on my face. He came toward me ready to punch me. I hastily walked back into my apartment and he followed right along. Finally I said the words, "I am your friend," and that, miraculously, made the man turn around and go back to his scuffle in the hallway.

I quickly locked the door and never dared to do that foolish act ever again. Once I was safely in, every day after school, I stayed put until the next day. Even if they had social events in a large space across from our building, we would play it safe and look from the distance, just in case.

One night I heard a man yelling outside in the distance. I remember that there what appeared to be a scuffle between two men, but it was dark and could not see clearly. The next morning the news stations announced that someone in the complex had beaten up a policeman who happened to be in the area alone. It must have been a nasty beating from someone much stronger than him, as the policeman was not able to pull out his gun and defend himself.

While we were there, there were no shootings and no murders. This was probably due to the low availability of guns, the significantly high police presence and, probably, the high number of immigrants who lived in the complex who cared only about surviving and saving enough so as to escape the nightmarish crucible of living in Government housing.

All of these events helped to create a vast amount of anxiety in me and my parents and, after probably a year and one half of enduring much tension and fear, my father fulfilled his dream: he bought a house near Little Italy, thus bringing the nightmare to a close.

While we were able to escape the public housing nightmare, a great many, including many poor immigrants, were left behind in that hellish environment with children that felt like I felt, or worse.

Some Government-housing complexes can be very scary places. The ones we have in Toronto have become dens for drug users and drug pushers. Unlike those days, killings are now frequent and sometimes innocent people are caught in the crossfire.

Yet, because of the high cost of rent, a great many immigrants end up having to leave in such dens of anxiety and fear. When I imagine the horror that young people must feel when they hear of shootings and murders happening next door to them or in their area, I feel deep feelings of sadness at their plight, which I somewhat tasted, many years ago.

The negative effect of those days on my mind lasted for quite some time. How long will the children living in government housing today will require to heal from their traumas, which are by far greater than what I ever experienced?

How long will the immigrant parents take to heal

when their children, sucked into the vortex of local gangs, end up becoming drug addicts or even drug dealers? How will those parents ever heal when their child is shot dead by opposing gangs? This is North America's gift to them; not the fulfillment of a dream but the ultimate nightmare.

CHAPTER 15 —

DEATH KNOCKS AT OUR DOOR

Within months of our stay in the Government-housing apartment a horrible event shook us and traumatized us. It happened very late at night. My mother woke me up around midnight looking quite afraid. My father had a pain in his left arm, which had become unbearable. I had to take him to the hospital. The thought of calling an ambulance never crossed our minds. It was just "a pain in the left arm."

I called a cab, but I was not overly concerned. We walked down to the entrance to wait for the cab to arrive. My father looked very pale and weak. His pain in the arm looked agonizing. He sat on the floor by the elevator. At that point I became very concerned. I felt totally helpless.

The cab finally came. My father sat at the back, and I asked the cab driver to take us to the hospital. While in the cab, the man looked at my father and immediately said: "This is serious." He pushed the pedal all the way to the Toronto Western Hospital where my father was taken into emergency immediately. I was asked to wait in the waiting area.

I waited probably for 15-20 minutes and then I saw an older policeman walk my way. He told me that I could go in and that my father "was having a heart attack."

My heart sank.

I walked to my father's room where he was connected to tubes and wires. My father looked alert. I told him what they told me. He was surprised, but did not seem to panic.

They kept him there for a while and then on to intensive care. I followed the stretcher to the ICU. I stayed with him for a while. I was informed that there was a possibility things could have turned for the worse, but that he would have been monitored closely. I had to go home and inform my mother. It was 2-3 O'clock in the morning. I had no money for a cab. I had to take a street car home, but at that hour they passed by infrequently. Fortunately, it was summer night.

After a long wait, the streetcar finally arrived. Soon I was back in our complex going to tell my concerned mother that my father was having a heart attack and that he could have died that very night.

We went to bed, but I prayed through the night. I heard my mother crying.

A few hours later, we went to the hospital relieved to find out that my father had survived. He actually looked lively and promising. He did not need an operation.

We were told that he would have had to stay in the hospital for a few days and that he would have then returned home. All looked promising, until pneumonia set in. His life was again in danger. Again he fought and won.

After two long weeks, he was back home but was unable to do much. He had to stop working for quite some time. My mother was also unemployed, because of serious health reasons. Things became bleak and scary in the Caputo residence.

Illness occasionally impedes the American dream. The stresses of a new life can take their toll. New foods,

polluted air and polluted water can have an adverse effect on new immigrants as well. Sometimes to speed up the way to success immigrants may end up doing what my father had done: he had gotten a second job which he would go to after returning from his regular one.

Strangely, after having his heart attack, he never again had problems with his heart. All seems to be indicative of the fact that holding two jobs may have been, at least in part, responsible for his nearly-deadly episode.

Nonetheless, such an experience can be quite overwhelming, as it definitely was for me and my parents.

CHAPTER 16 —

THE WELFARE EXPERIENCE

As mentioned above, suddenly we found ourselves in a terrible and scary predicament. We had no money and few savings. We did not want to become burdens on our extended family. It was time to go to the welfare office and seek help, and I was the one who would do it.

The lady I spoke with was quite sympathetic. She acknowledged that Italians did not readily seek welfare help and that they preferred to work.

I believe we received some help for a few weeks, after which my father went back to work. My mother got better and found a job within walking distance of our building. She got a job cutting old clothes. It was dirty job, as some of the materials she cut were filthy and at times bloody. What the factory ended up doing with the parts was not clear.

One of the benefits of working in that factory is that my mother brought home some second-hand pants and other items which were quite wearable, once washed. I wore some of those clothes for years.

Welfare was the ultimate shame in our community, and I suppose it is so also for members of some other immigrant communities. Some immigrants, unfortunately, seek it gladly and pay the consequence of becoming addicted to easy living and end up never going far in life. Based on my observations, most immigrants evade it and move on to working for their livelihood and are glad they made the right choice.

CHAPTER 17 —

THE OTHER ENEMY OF SUCCESS

My uncle Rocco came to Canada in 1955. He lived in Montreal for three months but soon found out that work in that city was scarce. Uncle Rocco was a mentally strong man. He had been trained in the army and little scared him, even if it meant leaving the family and going to Toronto where he had little support.

There he sought and found. He was hired by a Jewish lumber yard owner and worked there for twelve years where he became appreciated and respected.

Within a year, he was joined by his love, Nina, who he

had married by proxy. The two lived and raised a special family in Toronto, Ontario.

Unfortunately, not very long after, Aunt Nina started showing worrisome signs. Rheumatic fever set in. It was soon concluded that she needed a heart-bypass operation.

Aunt Nina got better and was able to have three children: Michael, Angela and Palma. Aunt Nina's father and mother moved to Canada and they lived in the second-floor flat of the same house where they were able to help in a very difficult situation.

In time Uncle Rocco found a job as a cleaner in the famed Simpsons store in downtown Toronto. Aunt Nina's heart problems returned and she had to have another operation. The job required him to work at night.

Aunt Nina became very weak and the heart problems became frequent. Uncle Rocco had to take her to the nearby hospital regularly where she would stay for 2-3 days at a time. He helped with the cooking and the cleaning. Grandma upstairs helped as well.

He worked in the Simpsons store for fifteen years. Later on, he worked in a hospital for ten years. While working very hard at night, he helped make his wife's load as easy as he could. Zia endured her crucible with incredible patience. Zia Nina died peacefully in bed at age 79.

For my uncle and aunt the hopes of a joyful future in "America" became framed with incredible difficulties and challenges. But Uncle Rocco and Aunt Nina did not despair. They took what came their way with incredible courage and resilience. Amazingly, they did quite well financially as well.

They both succeeded in raising three very fine children. Michael, the oldest, holds a top position in the Ministry of Public Health, in Toronto. Angela married a successful electrician who owns his own business. Palma is a co-owner of an international transportation company. Remarkably, the anxieties and limitations in their home did not prevent them from achieving their goals.

Uncle Rocco was always an amazing man that never allowed tribulations to knock him down. His philosophy— was and still is—that in life one had to be "tough." Still, today, he is showing his toughness by living alone in his house while tackling significant health issues. He is truly a remarkable man.

Most certainly many immigrants end up being faced by similar circumstances, once in "America." They,

no doubt, appreciate the wonderful medical services, the welfare support, if needed, but their dream to a fast and successful future gets severely impeded by ill health. They are the ones who simply *survive* in "America" while the many others – friends and relatives – move ahead and achieve their dream. They are amazing people, nonetheless, who are deserving of much admiration.

Zio Rocco, Zia Nina, Mike and and Angela. Sweet Palma was yet to be born.

CHAPTER 18 —

A DREAM FULFILLED

For about two years, my father worked in very fine barber shops making very good money. Because his clients loved his hair cuts, they rewarded him with sizeable tips. The money coming in was plentiful, but the dream of owning a barber shop was yet in the future.

That frustration ended when one day, while passing by a barber shop near our house, he decided that it was time to make a move.

The barber shop was located right across from the Ossington subway station, a location which should have made the barber shop a gold mine, yet it seemed to be always empty. The older Italian barber simply did not seem to attract much of a clientele. My father, though, concluded that he could turn the business around. He had the skills; he had the personality and the location was prime.

So my father went in the shop and convinced the old man to sell it to him at a decent price. Soon after my father took over, he changed the sign, made the inside more appealing and left the rest to his skills and personality. Within months my father's barber shop was full and, at one point he ended up employing two other barbers. His dream was now fulfilled and he started reaping of the fruit of the high tree called "America."

From that point on money poured into his pockets in large quantities. He was now one of the "successful ones" and never again craved to move back to Italy.

Finally owing a business is the turning point for many immigrants. Whether it's a restaurant, a variety store, a cab or a construction-related business, once that stage is reached, immigrants will do their utmost to make it succeed. They will work extra hard. They will work seven days a week. They will sleep just a few hours and few will fail and if they will fail they will try again and again until the dream of success is finally reached.

And if perchance they cannot start a business, they will work extra hard in factories or construction; they will hold a second job, if they have to, and they will sacrifice and save and save, so as to send their children to university so that the much-craved success is achieved *vicariously* through them, if that is all that is possible.

Ossington Barbershop, right across from a subway station and next door to Toronto's Bloor street, one of the two busiest streets in Toronto. Antonio was certain it would have become a success—and it did.

CHAPTER 19 —

THE CONSTRUCTION BOOM

Few Italian immigrants that came to Canada had ever worked in construction. Most were tough agricultural workers who had eked a living from small plots of land and who were not afraid of hard physical labor, overtime and weekend work. They had done that for years and their bodies were accustomed to that kind of punishment.

In Canada there was little agricultural work, except for the few who moved to the Windsor area where tomato farms abounded. The place where they could employ their toughness and make a lot of money was construction.

Both Montreal and Toronto were booming, in part thanks to the tens of thousands of immigrants that were yearly pouring into both cities. Houses had to be built for them. New roads had to be paved. Sewers had to be dug and pipes had to be laid. The money paid was high and the payment was regular. Thousands poured into that field and worked long hours and did weekend work—*gladly*.

With the money they made, they bought a house in what became the Little Italies of today. The wives worked mostly in factories and added to the wealth that poured in. Most had never seen so much money. Their frugality, their willingness to rent the upstairs flat or part of the basement to strangers and the money they worked so hard for did something that most Canadians had never been able to do: pay off the mortgage in just a few years (My parents did so in three and one half years).

HOW TO PAY A MORTGAGE—FAST!

Most Italians in Toronto bought three story houses with two flats, which they turned into small apartments. The plan was simple: stay on the first floor and rent out both the second and third floors to different tenants. Some even rented a portion of their basement.

We kept the basement but rented out the second and third floor, which my father had turned into comfortable, modern-looking apartments. The entrance was common for all of us, but we did not care about privacy. What we cared about was to sacrifice temporarily, so as to finally move to a private home.

Of course one does not know what kind of people come in. We had a foreigner who lived on the third floor who regularly brought in his girl friend but not for any holy activities. The man, unfortunately, ended up stealing from a Japanese tenant who lived on the first floor.

We also had a couple who loved their drinks. The wife was so drunk one day that she carried her plentiful body outside totally naked, while her husband was desperately trying to get her back inside.

I also remember a grandmother, her daughter and her granddaughter who rented out both floors. They were gentle souls who were probably surviving on a pension and welfare.

I also remember a European father and son in his twenties who probably worked in construction. The son was a ladies' man and started seducing a young married woman who lived next door. He may have succeeded, as I saw her come out of his car one day, not far from my father's barbershop. I know he weekly groomed himself for his weekend encounter with ladies of the night, which he visited faithfully.

We also welcomed a young Italian couple by the name of Versace. The husband, as I recall, was the cousin of the Versace stylist who created the Versace brand. In fact, there was a definite resemblance.

Lastly, I cannot forget Jim, a Greek man probably in his forties, who one day disappeared. Not long after, we were informed by a social worker that Jim was a schizophrenic and had been hospitalized in the nearby mental-health centre. As I recall, he had attacked a customer in a store.

Needless to say, we asked that Jim's very few possessions be picked up and we rented the flat immediately to someone else. The thought that we had actually had the man in our house that was somewhat dangerous was quite disconcerting, but those were the risks my father was willing to take to pay off his house–and he did.

Finally, my father and countless others, after paying

off their mortgage they moved to single-family homes and never again rented any part of their homes to anyone. A number continued renting out their second floor or their basement, if they had a separate entrance, and many of their children and grandchildren are today following their grandparent's examples so as to accomplish the same aim.

The first house bought by my parents. Renting out the second and third floor was one factor that led to the payment of the mortgage in just over three years.

CHAPTER 20

WHEN DEATH KILLED THE DREAM

Most immigrants who land in Canada will achieve a level of success if they work hard and are willing to sacrifice. Some, who also worked very hard, were confronted with a fierce enemy that shattered their dreams. The enemy was death.

My uncle Philip achieved much and became very prosperous. He and his wife Lisa worked very hard for many years. They had two children, both quite intelligent and very promising. The daughter, Josephine, once mature, worked her way to becoming a bank manager with a major Canadian bank.

Michael was also very bright and would have, no doubt achieved much in life, had it not been with a battle with leukemia which finally took his life in his early teen years. My uncle and wife did well financially but had to carry the horrendous burden of the great loss of their son until the end of their days.

My in-laws also shared with me the story of a couple who came to Canada, had some children and was able to start a business which, I believe, was a variety store.

Unfortunately the husband developed cancer. The horrible disease became a crucible which led to their being unable to keep their store which in turn led to severe financial stress. I am told that they sought welfare assistance but were refused. Unable to confront the expenses that death would have brought about, the man left his family and went to die back in his Italian home town.

ZIA FRANCA'S TRAGEDY

Aunt Franca was a most likeable person. She was adored by my wife who was very close to her. She was my mother-in-law Julia's younger sister.

Franca had come to Canada, not long after Julia. She met Cosimo and got married. Together they had two children.

Zia Franca became a very successful hair stylist. Cosimo was a top-notch carpenter. Together they bought a big house in Woodbridge, the Italian upper class area of Toronto. "Zio Mimi'" as he was affectionately called, built himself a large and beautiful cottage near a lake, not far from Toronto.

Canada had been truly the land of fulfilled dreams for Franca and Mimi', until one night in 1979 when Franca was struggling to get home during a fierce Canadian blizzard.

Franca was stuck behind a snow plow and suddenly she was tempted to pass it. That was a tragic decision. Another car was coming from the opposite direction that somehow she had not seen. The two cars hit each other and Franca was killed instantly.

Suddenly the Canadian dream came to a sudden agonizing halt for Zia Franca and her family. The pain of the event is still with my wife and her family, and for me who greatly admired Zia Franca.

*Franca Tedesco:
A truly special human
being, for whom the
Canadian dream was
short-lived.*

THE HOG'S HOLLOW DISASTER

Pasquale Allegrezza, Giovanni Correglio, Giovanni Fusillo, Alessandro Mantella, and Guido Mantella had come to Canada ready to pursue the dream of financial success. They were willing to do the most risky jobs to get there.

March 17, 1960, they were working inside the water main under the Don River. This was dangerous work and safety measures were lax.

While working a fire started. Most of the workers escaped. The five men listed above were trapped inside and died a most horrific death, while yelling for help and begging for divine intervention.

The event was most tragic for the workers who died in the tunnel, for their families who suddenly found themselves without a breadwinner and for the thousands of Italian construction workers who suddenly realized that those who employed them did not necessarily have their welfare at heart.

Fortunately, a great many from the Italian community and from other communities came to the rescue and a lot of money was collected to help the victims' wives and children.

Ironically, thanks to that tragic event stringent labor laws were soon passed which made the life of workers much safer. It is quite unfortunate that it took the horrific death of five Italian immigrants to accomplish that.

A MONUMENT TO ITALIANS WHO DIED ON THE JOB

Though the work conditions, especially in construction sites, have improved significantly since the Hog's Hollow disaster, very lax work-safety laws over the past century have led to the death of over 1000 Italian workers.

To commemorate the sacrifices of these immigrants a

monument was inaugurated in 2019 in Toronto, which lists the names, birth date and date of death of each worker who died on a work site. The design allows for future casualties to be added.

I have recently gone to visit the monument and I am making some pictures I took available to the reader. This is my very limited way of honoring a great many special people and their families.

Please remember that the consequence of each tragic death was the loss of, in most cases, a breadwinner, a father, a husband, a child, a brother and a friend.

Also imagine the agony that each death caused and the long-term ramifications for the remaining family members. In each case the sought-after Canadian dream of financial security was shattered and want replaced it, especially in past decades when the social safety net was minimal or nonexistent.

Monument to Italian workers who died on Canadian work sites since 1900.

New names are being added to the monument, as made available.

CHAPTER 21 —

CHEATED OF THEIR FULL POTENTIAL

Many immigrants brought families along with young children. In many cases the children were approaching the teen years. Some were teenagers. Their knowledge of English was nil. The little ones learned quickly and lost their accent; the ones that entered grades six to ten were at a big disadvantage. High school was approaching and their English was poor or quite weak.

By the end of grade eight, the school decided if you would go to an academic school or a business school to learn secretarial skills, if you were a girl, or if you would end up in a trade school, if you were a boy.

Of the young Italian ladies whose knowledge of English was limited, a great many ended up in the two business schools in the area; a great many boys ended up in an infamous trade school, not very far from where I lived.

I was asked by my teacher what I wanted to do, and I answered that I wanted to go to an art high school to become a commercial artist. That was not a problem, since an advanced knowledge of English was not really a requirement. That saved me from the infamous trade school where some of my friends ended up.

My Italian friends were bright and energetic and could have done wonderful things had they been given the time to learn the language well. Some went to the high school, became bored, quit and went to work.

Because of their resourceful spirit, some became successful in business, while others settled in manual labor where they did well nonetheless, but much talent and brain power was lost because the government was not really concerned about their potential and their future.

Incidentally, that problem became a concern to Pierre

Berton, a famed Canadian writer and TV interviewer, who, I remember clearly, interviewed one such student and scolded the authorities for wasting such potential. That, and other factors, may have led to significant changes in the system, which appear to have benefited the many other young immigrants that came to Canada ever since.

CHAPTER 22 —

ITALIAN MEDIA IN CANADA

Oh, how much immigrants ached for back home. Oh, how much we longed to see our families, our friends, our streets and to listen to our music.

Some enterprising Italian-Canadians saw the need and satisfied it by creating either short Italian programs on local TV or radio stations. As mentioned above, Johnny Lombardi, in 1966, created CHIN which would broadcast in Italian until sunset on AM radio and then it would pick up on FM until sunset until late hours.

On Sunday Emilio Mascia, an Italian from Hamilton, a small city near Toronto, gave us visual treats directly from

Italy adding the cream to the cake. CHIN later on added Italian TV broadcasting, further enriching the weekends with Italian visual treats.

CHIN, to the bliss by importing great Italian stars. Huge crowds would pack local stadiums, savoring every song and loving to have their favorite stars right in front of them – something which most of them would have never have been able to afford back home.

Another great gift to the community was the creation of Italian newspapers. The two most successful ones were, "Il Sole," which died out long ago and the "Corriere Canadese," which appears to be still thriving with a digital edition now added.

This pattern is now being followed by the many other ethnicities which live in Southern Ontario, except that what is made available is much more plentiful than what we had. This helps to lessen the nostalgia and makes the long Canadian winter days so much more bearable.

The future is not promising, though, since the large number of first-generation Italian readers is slowly dying out. The new generation gets its news from the Internet, thus making local papers redundant.

CHIN Radio began as a tiny station in Little Italy, serving primarily the Italian community. Today it transmits, from this impressive building, in over thirty languages. This much-loved station is today being managed by Johnny Lombardi's children.

CHAPTER 23 —

THE

UNFORGETTABLE

WEDDINGS

Weddings became an opportunity for Italian immigrants to show that they had reached a high financial status among the community; therefore much money was spent for the event.

The job of making the wedding a success was handed over to one well-known Italian caterer who had proven himself with several other weddings. He would be the one to provide the hall, the food, the flowers (through connections) and the "bomboniere" (small gifts given out at the end of the wedding as a memento of the occasion.)

Young, local Italian kids provided the entertainment. They were young hopefuls who were, in their minds, on their way to becoming great stars. The group I chose to play for us at our wedding happened to be led by a young man I had gone to high school with.

The food was abundant; the courses were many. Attendees, of course, brought all or some of their children with them, as a feast without children was no feast. Of course, soon parents were busy reconnecting with friend and relatives and the children were left to themselves running around and becoming a bit of a nightmare for waiters and waitresses. Fortunately, servers were very attentive and accidents, miraculously, were few, but announcements were regularly made to keep the kids at the table with not-always-successful results.

Normally the number of attendees ranged from 300 to 400. Over 400 attended our wedding. Many years later, a friend had over 500 attendees. It was a sea of people.

Weddings started late. The invitation stated clearly that the meal would begin at seven, but, invariably, time would drag on and start time would be one to two hours late, to make sure that all the invited relatives and friends were present. Some who were busy talking, snacking and drinking barely took notice of the passing time, some others who were hungry tended to get quite irritated.

Then the food poured in. The first course was the "antipasto" (the appetizer): olives, sliced meats, cheeses, artichokes or other combinations. This was meant to stimulate the appetite but, often, it filled our stomach and made the mountain of food to come more challenging to indulge in.

Then came, "Il secondo," the second dish: rice and/or pasta. Sometimes two pasta dishes were served, one with cream and the other with a delectable tomato sauce. Parmesan was poured on in abundance.

Then came the meats and the vegetables – two meats, and a copious amount of vegetables, potatoes and salad. All was concluded with one or two desserts—usually a "tartufo"—a well-known Italian ice cream, and a slice of cake.

Red and white wine was on the table free for the taking and alcoholic and non-alcoholic beverages were there for the asking – *without limit.*

Afterwards the music and the dancing began. Lots of

fun Italian dance classics were played with some North American music thrown in. The fun was unforgettable and joy abounded throughout the night.

Then more food. Pizza and sandwiches arrived by 11:00 p.m. or so and, on occasion – and now apparently quite common – a roasted pig was made available for the hungry types who by 1-2:00 a.m. were still ready to add to their already-packed stomachs.

Our weddings of those days were truly memorable and the joy of the night is still chiseled in the many participants' hearts.

But with the second and third generations things have changed quite noticeably.

Weddings start closer to the announced time. The background music is often not a joyful sound, but a repetitive, loud beat that can get quite annoying. The numbers have dropped dramatically. In my experience 100-200 is now typical. Children are few, as it lowers the cost of attending. The Italian-style appetizer is still there. The courses are fewer and the plates are more artistic–but less abundant. All is concluded with a simple slice of cake or an ice cream. People are more proper and the high level of exuberance is no longer there.

The most odious thing that I have had to bear, for several years now, is the very loud, modern music, which prevents discussion and which invariably leads me, my wife and other old timers to leave early, so as to protect our ear drums. Complaining is of no use. The young love the music and the musicians or disk jockeys care not about us older ones. Overall the experience is mediocre and in my view deteriorating, as marriage loses the value and sanctity it once had.

On occasion, nowadays, one goes to a second marriage or even a third marriage, as I saw a few years ago when my daughter's friend married an older man who had been married twice before.

I looked at the faces of the groom's family and I saw sadness instead of joy. They had seen their close relative go through two previous celebrations, two previous vows, two previous sets of speeches framed with eternal love, and they participated as if at a funeral. This is the new reality occasionally present in the Canadian-Italian community, which is very hard for us who came from Italy to even comprehend, let alone accept.

This is also the reality other marriage-loving immigrant communities had to get used to–*painfully*.

Unlike the simpler weddings of the past, today's Italian-Canadian weddings are very luxurious and elegant. Food quantity and joyful music have been replaced with an emphasis on the visual impact and the old melodious music has been replaced with modern music which is far from appealing to the remaining first and second generation

CHAPTER 24 —

ACCEPTING THE UNACCEPTABLE

MARRIAGE, SACRED – DIVORCE, UNTHINKABLE

Since early age, the Catholic Church inculcated in its members that marriage was for life–*no matter what.* If there was abuse involved, you were allowed to seek some respite at relatives' places for awhile but, later, you had to get back home and work out your differences.

My mother recounted, more than once, that after she got married to my father there were some heated arguments. They must have been quite hot, given my father's initial tendency toward authoritarianism and my mother's determined response which yelled loud and clear: "Not with me, buddy!"

This led to some pretty intense altercations, and one day my mother decided to teach my father a lesson and went back home, thinking that she would have had the immediate support of her family. But my grandfather responded quite differently: *he ordered her* to get back home and sort out her differences. She had no choice but do so.

There is a sacred Italian proverb which goes as follows: "Fra moglie e marito non mettere un dito" (Do not stick one finger between a man and his wife). In other words, stay out of a man and his wife's affairs–and that applies to relatives as well. Even if they would listen and commiserate, the final suggestion was invariably, "Try your best to make things better."

In those distant days, divorce was not a possibility and as an older person once (I vaguely remember it being my grandmother) said to someone who mentioned it jokingly: "That's a word that should not ever be mentioned."

Well, that has changed both here and in Italy. The divorce rate is slowly climbing in the old country, and it is slowly climbing in the Canadian-Italian community.

Southern Italians, though, are not as prone to divorce as Northern Italians, but there is an increase among them as well.

Divorces are painful to all, of course, but to the first generation of Italians that landed in Canada, it is shattering. Having to accept the end of something sacred that started so joyfully and with so much promise and hope, is nothing short of agonizing – especially if children are involved.

I doubt that there are many Canadian-Italian homes (or other immigrant communities) that have not been yet touched by the anguish of divorce. The agony, unfortunately, continues.

COMMON LAW LIVING

As I recall, in the upper limits of my Italian town lived a man, a woman and their several children. Beside the fact that the man was often drunk, what also was well known about that family is that the man and the woman were not married. The town had accepted the partnership, but all knew that "they were living in sin."

That attitude was quite pervasive within the very

Catholic Italian community. Living common-law was simply unacceptable. You were supposed to make a commitment to one partner *forever* – "for better or for worse." The idea of living together before marriage would have made a woman a whore and the man would have received little respect. You were supposed to get married to the one you loved and you were to stay married–*period!*

Times have changed in this regard in both Canada and in Italy. Though in Southern Italy the numbers who live common law are relatively few in comparison to North America and Northern Italy, the attitude toward common-law arrangements is changing dramatically.

Italians and other conservative immigrants who came a few decades ago watch their children gravitate toward these news modes of operating–and cringe. Sometimes they are just plain forced to accept their children rebelling against their parents' ways, but do so with much suffering. Often the battles may have been quite intense, but the children declared their independence and did what they wanted, while the parents often accepted the defeat *–and the shame.*

Some may have even cursed the day they came to this country, given the embarrassment that they would

have had to endure in their family and community.

MARRYING NON-ITALIANS

Another great adaptation was having to accept their child marrying someone from another ethnic group or race. First-generation Italians prefer to maintain the Italian lineage by encouraging their children to marry someone within the Italian community. Even a half Italian would do. Unfortunately their children attended schools where they met young people from other ethnic backgrounds and races and when they fell in love with non-Italians, parents had to adapt to a new reality.

Many such relationships still retained one similarity: the Catholic faith and that helped to soften the blow. Some did not and that made the arrangement hard to take–unless the boy-friend proved to be a "nice" person. Sincere charm would have been accepted as a sufficient replacement, if the other factors were missing.

Today we have a large number of Canadian Italians who have intermarried. I have cousins that have married terrific Anglo-Canadians, one married a wonderful French-Canadian and one married a very special Chinese-Canadian. In all cases the marriages

proved to be made in heaven and the children that were born from these relationships are nothing short of wonderful.

NON-CATHOLIC RELIGIONS – HARD TO ACCEPT

Italians have a powerful attachment to their Catholic faith. It gives them direction in this life, strength during difficult times and hope for the future. Back in Italy, there was "one, true faith" and it was dictated by the Pope, whom many Italians still revere.

Coming to Canada opened the curtain to not only other Christian faiths but also to Asian faiths which to them were strange and incomprehensible. Marrying a person from another ethnic group was difficult to accept but seeing a child leave the faith of their ancestors behind was simply heartbreaking, especially if they were quite distant from the beliefs and customs of the Catholic Church.

I remember when my best, high-school friend, Mario, started delving into an Easter religion and, finally, started practicing it. When his Southern-Italian parents found out, they entered a panic mode and did their utmost to free their son from what they saw as religious monster. They even begged me to try to do something about it, but I could do little, given Mario's obsession with the new way.

I also remember a young man who moved toward a Christian group that kept many of the Jewish customs (Saturday instead of Sunday, and the Jewish Holy Days instead of Christmas and Easter). The father became enraged at the fact that the son had become "a Jew" (which was not the case), and insisted in fury that "no Italian should become a Jew. You must stay Italian!"

To the man changing religion was committing a double sin. The son was leaving his ethnic roots and the faith of his forefathers. The young man stood firm and to this day practices his new faith, while being a very successful human being. His parents finally accepted but did not – ever – celebrate his change.

Many years ago, I worked with a young lady of a non-Christian faith. She fell in love with a Catholic-Italian and the result was great strain within the young lady's family. All the anger and the threats did not succeed in preventing her from marrying the one she loved. As a result, she was shunned by the family and was rejected as a daughter.

I dare not judge nor condemn the young lady's parents.

They come from a background where their faith has been central to everything they are for millennia. Their Holy Book forbids any such marriages and, therefore, from the parents' perspective, the young lady was not just offending her parents, she was offending God; thus, the *seemingly* disproportioned reaction and the painful results for both the young lady and her family.

Encounters with new religions, such as the three examples mentioned above, are a great trauma that very few immigrants are ready for and, when the challenge comes their way, it truly causes great distress for all involved.

I am sure that some of the honor killings that have taken place among some very conservative, immigrant communities have been the result of young ladies falling in love with someone outside of their faith. In some communities marrying someone outside of the faith is a shameful sign of failure for the parents and brothers and in some extreme cases to atone for the daughter's sin a human sacrifice takes place, so as to regain respect within the community, which is hard for us Westerners to comprehend and accept but is the demanded reaction within some communities.

Some young people who are pulled out of their ethnic group and/or faith end up seeking help. Their parents, who also enter a period of great stress, whose mental health is also affected, tend to keep their anguish inside and vent only with close family members, which may not be at all sufficient.

Italians have had to accept this reality as well. The fact that most of their children attend Catholic high-schools leads to their bonding and later marrying young people from other ethnic groups who happen to also be Catholics. This helps cushion the blow and, therefore, many Italians have married Irish, Germans, South Americans and even Philipinos who go to the same churches, have the same Savior, worship the same God, revere Mary and pray to the same saints.

CHAPTER 25 —

THE CURSE OF DRUGS

Drugs were unheard of where most Italian immigrants came from. People struggled daily with survival and escaping the challenges of life was done with drinking wine and spending time with family and friends.

Drugs worked their way into the Italian-Canadian community gradually and created a new and terrifying experience immigrant parents were simply not equipped to handle.

Young people were introduced to drugs in their schools and many joined in to escape psychological pain, though some did simply to fit in with cool groups of friends. Most of such young people had no idea what they were getting themselves into. The results were slavery to a taskmaster that will not relent, once in control.

In some cases, the drug use led to severe mental illness, such as the case of a teenager I counseled years ago who only abused Cannabis. Because of his weak nervous system, he developed schizophrenia and stayed with schizophrenia for the rest of his life. I worked with this young man as a therapist. I also counseled the mother, a beautiful and intelligent woman, who was overwhelmed with his son's illness. I saw the change in her face and how the stress of the situation transformed her into a much-older-looking woman within three to four short years.

Another family lost three boys to drugs. All three died of drug overdose, as I recall. The parents had worked hard to build a future for their children; instead they lived to bury them in a foreign land.

The drug problem in the Italian community in Toronto is sizeable. A wonderful lady and a priest have created a treatment centre, just outside of the city. The success statistics appear to be significant, as the centre has been around for a long time and continues to thrive.

Others send their children to treatment centers in Italy. The success rate for such cases I do not know, but I have heard of a case recently for who much money was spent and the man, now an older adult, is still very much addicted.

This painful reality is mirrored in all ethnic communities. The agony which follows drug use is the same for all parents who see their children waste away while slaves to drugs. They never would have imagined that "The Promised Land" would have become, instead, a house of horrors.

CHAPTER 26—

CRIMINALS TAKE A FOOTHOLD

Crime was almost non-existent in Toronto, and especially in our Italian community. Work abounded and Italians were too busy making money honestly to need to turn to crime.

Unfortunately, in time, it became obvious that a few among us favored the evil ways rather than the ways of honesty.

I believe in the early seventies the owner of a well-known travel agency organized a charter flight to Italy for probably 200-300 Italians. The cost was quite affordable and the flight was full.

Unfortunately, once the flight reached capacity the agency owner took a flight, probably to South America, and disappeared, with hundreds of thousands of dollars in his pockets. The Community was shocked. Unfortunately it became obvious that they were not safe from scamming criminals even in Canada.

Probably in the eighties the owner of CHIN Radio, the much loved Italian radio station, received a letter in which he was told that he had to pay a certain amount of money or be killed. The man who sent the letter was traced and was arrested.

In the mid-eighties a popular series was shown on Canadian TV. The series gave evidence that some Southern-Italian crime families had established themselves in Canada and that their criminal activities were flourishing and growing. It became then obvious that the cancer which we thought had been left behind had followed us to the land of plenty. This only served to strengthen the unfortunate stereotype that Italians are Mafiosi.

CHAPTER 27 —

ON TO HIGH SCHOOL AND BEYOND...

Then the end of the year came. The grade eight teacher asked me which school I wanted to go to. This was a turning point in my life and I didn't know it. I was not ready to move on to an academic high school. My English was still quite limited. Other kids in my situation were sent to vocational schools. I escaped the same fate by telling the teacher I wanted to go to Central Technical School, to be in the art program and become an artist. That was OK with her.

Those were two of the most wonderful years of my life. Though some academic course where included, the emphasis was mostly art, an area in which I had grown to excel.

Several Italian kids went there, as well as kids from other backgrounds. In our class there was a very talented Greek boy, two Portuguese kids, a Czechoslovakian blonde, a Portuguese young lady and a Chinese young woman who quit the program, once she had to look at the first naked model.

The teachers were outstanding. Mrs. Green was a paper artist who could produce the most incredible art works with paper. Mrs. Davis, a lovely older woman, supervised the figure drawing course and two gentlemen took care of the rest. One such male teacher was upsetting because she insisted that I could not have done some drawings, because they were of too high a quality to be drawn by someone in grade ten. He was wrong!

Cannabis was being used by some of the Canadian students, but I and my other ethnic friends saw no need for it. We just spent a lot of time together and our social time was more than rewarding and joyful. We had no need for what we saw as dangerous substances. Furthermore, our healthy fear of our parents helped to reinforce our resistance to any temptation.

Once it became obvious that the only path I could take after the four year program was the local art college and that I could not go to university to pursue an art degree which would have allowed me to teach art, I decided to switch to a collegiate which would have paved my way to my dream.

After two years at Central Tech, I moved to Oakwood Collegiate. Then two years at a liberal arts college in Pasadena, California. Pollution forced me to return and enroll at York University in Psychology where I would pursue my newfound dream of becoming a psychologist.

While at York, I met my gorgeous wife, Leonilda, a stunning Central-Italian young lady who also spoke Italian fluently.

My first counseling job came nine months after graduation at the Youth Clinical Services, affiliated to York-Finch Hospital. There I counseled disturbed young people and their families.

Soon after, I married Leonilda and two years later our first child was born, Anthony, was followed by Julie, our only girl. While working at YCS, I also finished a Masters' in counseling in three years of part-time studies.

Three years in Rome, Italy, followed and Victor was

born. At the end of the three years, we returned to Toronto when I decided to move into education. I worked for the Peel Board of Education as a teacher and as a counselor for nearly two decades. I also taught psychology at Toronto's Seneca College for almost the same amount of time. During that very fulfilling time, Leonilda and I bought a new comfortable home in the suburbs where we raised our precious children. Life was good.

Things went well for me and my family. We first lived in a fine condo, and then moved to a small house. Finally we bought a beautiful house in the suburbs where we have been living for three decades.

Professionally I have done what I love doing for decades at both the high school and college level. I have written various books some of which have been quite successful. My wife and I have done a lot of traveling.

I doubt that all of these opportunities would have come my way in a small and poor village in Southern Italy. I thank God for all His many blessings and for my parents who fortunately decided long ago to make the risky move from Italy to "America."

Our family is now into the fourth generation. If my

parents were alive they would have enjoyed seeing their great grand-children and would have rejoiced at the fact that they will have a promising future in a land of plenty.

Grazie mamma e papa' per tutti i vostri sacrifici e per il vostro grande amore. (Thank you mom and dad for all your sacrifices and your great love). This statement of gratitude applies to my father-in-law, Vittorio, and my precious mother-in-law, Julia, as well. This book will make sure that your challenging days, your anxious and difficult times and your courage and resilience will never be forgotten by all who will have your genes embedded in their own.

WHEN WE CAME TO AMERICA

CONCLUSION

Looking back over half a century, it is quite clear that my parents' decision to move to Canada was a very good one for them and for both me and my sister. Both siblings are now eating the fruits of the very high tree, thanks to my parents' hard work, frugality, risk-taking—*and resilience.*

This is what it takes to reach the top of the tree. All who adopt these principles have a very high probability of success.

My suggestion to all who reach our shores is to be patient—*and never give in.* The challenges will be many, but they are not insurmountable. The rewards will be many as well. Millions have experienced the difficulties followed by the ultimate successes.

Just stay fixed on the top of the tree, for the fruits will finally be yours, if you persevere and *never relent.* That is the great lesson I hope this book has taught the reader.

May you climb high, therefore, and may you achieve much success. Many others have done it—<u>and so will you</u>!

Surrounded by close relatives, including great-grand-children, Antonio and Teresa Caputo celebrate their fiftieth wedding anniversary. This celebration also marked the culmination of close to four successful decades in Canada. Antonio and Teresa are very grateful for having tackled the challenges and for having overcome the barriers My sister, Maria and I joined them in the celebration, as grateful beneficiaries of their success.

Vittorio and Julia Checca and their daughter, Leonilda, my wife, also celebrating their fiftieth wedding anniversary. The path to success was long and difficult, but they, too, succeeded in reaching the dream they sought after in "America."

My children, my wife and I, as we looked several years ago. Anthony (top), Victor and Julie are now successful professionals in their chosen fields. They have followed the example of hard work instilled in them by their grand-parents and their parents. They have and will continue to reap the blessings left behind by their self-sacrificing progenitors.

Anthony and Ivana's children, Matthew, Daniel, Michaela and Ava, as they look in 2019. They represent the fourth generation of Caputos that descend from four courageous and very hard-working grand-parents who came to Canada many years ago.

ABOUT THE AUTHOR

MICHAEL CAPUTO was born in the beautiful Region of Calabria, in Southern Italy, but has resided in Canada most of his life, with intervals in both Los Angeles and Rome, Italy. Michael holds a BA in Psychology, a Bachelor of Education, a Masters' Degree in Psychology and Education and several teaching qualifications. Michael taught and counseled at the high school level for over two decades, while teaching part time at the college level for sixteen years. Michael is the author of the award-winning book, *God Seen Through the Eyes of the Greatest Minds.* He is married to Leonilda and is the proud father of three special children: Anthony, Julie and Victor.

Manufactured by Amazon.ca
Acheson, AB

13109313R00094